THE MOTOLADY'S BOOK
OF WOMEN WHO RIDE

THE MOTOLADY'S BOOK
OF WOMEN WHO RIDE

MOTORCYCLE HEROES, TRAILBLAZERS & RECORD-BREAKERS

ALICIA MARIAH ELFVING

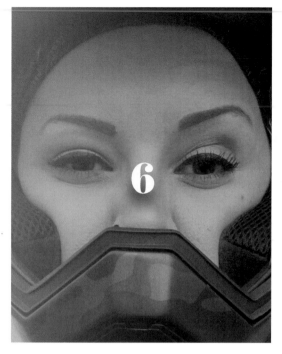

HOW IT STARTED During crazy-hot Portland days, my dad and I often would beat the heat by hanging out at restaurants and having a snack. I remember sitting at Denny's as a wee lass, watching the world go by through big windows. I pressed my hands against the glass to get a better view of a big rumbly cruiser (probably a Harley, let's be real) sitting at the stoplight across the street. The rider was geared up in leather from head to toe. "Isn't he hot?" I asked my dad.

Dad explained that oftentimes wearing a leather jacket protected you from sun and wind exposure, actually keeping you cooler while moving. To this day I have no idea if he's right about that, as I'm an ATGATT (all the gear all the time) rider, but I do know it was a formative day for me in the world of motorcycling and my future within it. Motorcycles, riders in full gear, Mad Max, armor, all of it inspired the style of gear I choose to protect my body with.

Over a decade later, just after turning eighteen, I signed up for the motorcycle endorsement class through my college. After just a few days of classes, I was the proud owner of a license to operate two-wheeled vehicles! A lifelong dream, previously denied by rules and regulations from family members,

finally achieved. It took me another five years to save up to buy my first bike, and at twenty-three I forked over $875 to some dude from Craigslist, taking home a beat-up 1980 Yamaha Maxim XJ650. I lovingly referred to the Maxim as Machafuko, which is Swahili for "chaos," a name I found all too fitting in the months following the purchase. Trials and tribulations began (more trials than tribulations), but I managed to keep it rolling enough to put on a fair amount of miles through that summer and the following winter, even riding on Christmas Eve when the sun popped out, in below-freezing conditions.

Buying a piece-of-crap bike is a sort of motorcyclist boot camp.

Questionable brakes, speedometers that are neither here nor there, dry-rotted tires that newbie-you thinks will get you through a couple months. Lofty goals of fixing it up yourself, knowing almost nothing mechanical. These are the stressful side effects of buying that POS. But you know what? I've struggled my way through a lot of bike fixes, learned many rough lessons through my time behind bars, and I wouldn't trade them for anything.

PRESS AND EXPERIENCE In the decade-plus since I started MotoLady, I have been fortunate to work with some amazing photographers, creators, riders, and publications. Through the years I've chosen projects not because they pay the bills, but because they make me happy. There have been a few favorites . . .

The GT-MotoLady MV Agusta build started with a conversation I had with my good friend Sofi Tsingos (featured in this book). I found her online years before, because of the custom motorcycle she was building and raffling off for charity. After we finally met and became close, we were chatting about our connections in the motorcycle industry, the reach we had between us, and how much good we could do in the way of raising money. A few weeks and some extensive planning later, we kicked off the GT-MotoLady project. MV Agusta sold us a lightly used 2014 Brutale 800 in exchange for the press and promotion of their badass bike, and we were off. After all was said and done, Sofi and I raised $25,000 for St. Jude Children's Hospital. I could not have even comprehended that type of project without Sofi in my life, and I'm thankful for her ongoing support and love.

When I worked at MotoCorsa, the nation's number one Ducati dealership, we did a photoshoot in 2012 for the release of the Ducati Panigale. Since we were going to be the first ones to get our hands on the actual bike, my boss, Arun Sharma, wanted to be ahead of the curve and capture tasteful pin-up style shots of a gorgeous woman on the bike. A lot of other companies had posted images of models spread-eagle atop new motorcycles for wallpapers, but that just wasn't helpful to anyone. So we did a Panigale shoot with model and ballerina Kylie Shea, starting in full gear and ending tastefully topless (while showing nothing explicit). Shortly thereafter, Arun and I sat together in a meeting talking about the press responses we had gotten and decided we needed to do a parody shoot. I said we should use guys instead, and he proposed the fellas from the shop. The images became world famous, featured on everything from CNN's live news broadcast and website to the front page of Reddit.

A few years later, in 2015, I was contacted by colleague Jamie Robinson from MotoGeo about a project for the American Motorcycle Association (AMA) Get Women Riding campaign. We worked on a short video piece talking about how I got started in motorcycling and the building of my custom Ducati Monster named "Pandora." This ended up being the cover feature for *American Motorcyclist* and the women's motorcycling feature issue.

While these three experiences were formative for me, my most significant experiences have been the opportunities I've been given to travel by motorcycle, receive hands-on training, and ride some fifty different bikes.

WOMEN'S MOTORCYCLE SHOW

MotoLady was founded in January 2011. Each January I threw an anniversary party. Year three was the release of my custom Ducati Monster. Year four was the Quality Control Helmet Show featuring six artists and twelve custom helmets. But I did something different for year five. Since the beginning of the MotoLady website, I had wanted to feature women who ride and encourage those who were thinking about riding. Oftentimes those I looked up to most were builders, fabricators, and racers. People who seemed to get a thrill from their two-wheeled experiences, similar yet different from the next. So in 2016, the MotoLady Five-Year Anniversary Party and Women's Motorcycle Show was the start of a whole new passion of mine.

Since that 2016 show, we've encountered a variety of roadblocks and rocket launches. In 2018, just thirteen minutes before the show was officially over and while announcing raffle winners, thirteen cop cars and two LAPD helicopters swarmed the event like we were in *Fast & Furious*. Standing in the courtyard surrounded by awesome custom bikes built by women and watching spotlights dance in the sky and light up the event space, I can't say it was the worst experience. Almost everyone raved about what an amazing night it was, despite not getting their prizes right away. The LAPD officers came in after the show had cleared out and admitted they anticipated street racing or some

sort of gang-style gathering. I ended up recording them saying, "The women's motorcycle show is pretty awesome." Overall I feel like it was a win.

The event itself is meant to celebrate women who ride, build, fabricate, race, travel, and so much

more. It's not just about chopping your bike down and doing a ground-up build. It's about altering your bike for your style of riding and sharing it with the world. Most women weren't raised with a wrench in their hand, so we need to show examples of what can be done with the will to learn, a little know-how, reference materials, and some elbow grease. Hell, that's almost all I've ever worked, and all I've ever had to work with.

HISTORY MAKERS

"IT MAY SEEM A LITTLE CRAZY TO WALK DIRECTLY
INTO THE LINE OF FIRE . . . THOSE WHO ARE
WILLING, ARE THOSE WHO ACHIEVE GREAT THINGS."
—JESSI COMBS

While almost every woman featured in this book has made—or is making—history in one way or another, those featured in this chapter have made undeniable impacts in the motorcycle industry: from the first woman to win a road-racing world championship to the surviving original members of the Motor Maids, the first recognized (and longest-running) women's motorcycle club in North America.

These forces of nature aren't just fast—they're fierce, oftentimes fearless, and will be forever remembered for their accomplishments. They give their all in everything they do, inspiring others to live their dreams and go for things that many people will tell them are unrealistic. Because that sort of attitude is old news in their worlds.

JESSI COMBS

JESSI COMBS. WHERE TO START? YOU WERE (past tense will forever feel surreal and wrong) a beautiful soul, a badass, and an incredible person. The impact you made with your work will live on. The passions you inflamed, the excitement you fueled, the smiles you created. They will echo in our hearts, in our memories, on art gallery walls, in pieces you created, on the grounds you raced. They will roar down the street in the vehicles you built.

You opened your shop to me when I needed a little love in life, reaching out your hand when most were closed fists. Sharing your most precious space and inviting me behind the curtain into a world most people never got to glimpse. A woman of strength and compassion, tenacity, and faith. You were always honest even when it was difficult . . . a rare and important quality.

I met Jessi sometime in mid-2015 at Born Free when my friend Sofi Tsingos of GT-Moto had flown in from Texas to work with her and Real Deal business partner Theresa Contreras. Jessi was fluttering about, talking to fans and friends, smiling, and doing her thing. A few months later we got together for a good old-fashioned girls' night, getting sushi, watching movies, and going to the store at midnight to buy a full roasted chicken. We devoured it. The giggles were endless.

With so many similarities in our personalities and preferences, I always felt like we were kindred spirits. Sort of take-no-shit types with expansive, soft hearts. A friend for life. A partner in crime. One that was far busier and cooler than I would ever be, but that didn't matter.

Jessi and Theresa invited me to be a part of the Real Deal demos at Chopperfest and Babes Ride Out, where they offered short class-like intros into trades such as welding, pinstriping, and, in my case, leathercraft. The number of women in line for demos at the Real Deal booth during Babes Ride Out surpassed every other in the area by far. Women eagerly waited for their chance to get their hands dirty and try something new. I just felt lucky to get to work beside Jessi and soak up her wisdom and can-do attitude.

One of my all-time favorite memories is taking the long route with Jessi, Theresa, and Sofi back home from Babes Ride Out in Joshua Tree that summer. Jessi on her Triumph Scrambler, Theresa on her bobbed-out Harley, Sofi on the KTM Duke 390, and me on a little Yamaha SR400. We had a blast. All of us had similar spirited riding styles. Twisties were fun in our four-long formation of badass babes. When we stopped in Big Bear and wandered through some shops, Jessi and I both ogled at fringed purses made of foxes. When we descended the mountain, we saw one of the best sunsets of our entire lives. I will never forget that trip.

Later, when some things went sideways in my life, Jessi offered me workspace in her beautiful Long Beach shop. With a larger dog, motorcycles, *and* tools, I was struggling to find a new place in Southern California where I could keep the pup and have garage space. Because of her generosity, I ended up moving into one of the coolest places I've ever lived just fifteen minutes from the shop. Life was good.

15

AUTHOR'S NOTE: *This piece is extremely strange for me to write. I told Jessi about writing this book when I saw her at Sturgis in July 2019. She witnessed my first minibike race and even sent me a video of me zipping around the barrels with an extreme face of focus that I'm sure made her giggle. Our friendship makes the process of writing this feel, well, different. I think about how many of the women in this book loved and even looked up to her, how many women's lives she impacted . . . It's for these reasons that this profile reads a bit differently.*

At the time I didn't fully realize the rarity of my situation—Jessi was not one to "let people in" or share the carefully built and curated shop space she'd been building for a decade. For the next year we got to know each other like roommates would, swapping tales of triumph and tribulation, laughing and crying together. The more we got to know each other, the more similarities we found. The more I respected and loved her. All the nights staying up late chatting about what we wanted out of the future, where we hoped to be in twenty years. It makes me tear up just thinking about everything she will never get to do. But I take some solace in knowing she lived more in her lifetime than most people do.

My time at the shop ended abruptly when I decided to move out of SoCal (out of everywhere, really) to build out my truck to go on a long road trip. She was a huge influence in this massive life change of mine. Her fierce love for adventure and new experiences, her ability to push through fear and harness it for good . . . they lit a fire in me and showed me the only thing standing in my way was me. Jessi didn't let anyone stand in her way. Ever. And she'd push through with a contagious smile.

I for sure know the Women's Motorcycle Show wouldn't have been so successful without her involvement, beginning with the first WMS in 2016, when she brought her custom Triumph to showcase. Year two she brought her Harley "Lilly." And in 2018–2019 she and Theresa brought the whole Real Deal setup (as well as their bikes), offering welding and pinstriping classes.

I'm thankful that I saw her in 2019 in her home state of South Dakota during the Sturgis Rally.

It was in the middle of the rally at Camp Zero, a rad little satellite Buffalo Chip camp spot with tepees, calvary tents, RV spaces, and a bar in a barn. I was fueled with adrenaline, sticky and sweaty from the humidity and blaring sun, hauling respective ass around the little barrel racing track on a minibike. My first race ever. I won. I slayed. I was over the moon.

As I looked up into the crowd disheveled and elated, she appeared in all white like an angel. Clean, pristine, and classy in a sea of dirty biker and Daisy Duke types. I admitted I was really stoked she'd witnessed my first real race ever, but lamenting that it took me until I was into my thirties to finally get a taste of racing. I was hooked. "I was watching you. You were gettin' it!" she said. I did a little shimmy of excitement, so proud to have her approval. "This might be the first race of many, honestly. I think I'm addicted now." "GOOD!" she exclaimed, "You should!" Her big shiny smile gleamed.

We spent the next couple minutes catching up about random life events, including her recent move, before work pulled us in separate directions. I thought later how I didn't even get to hug her goodbye, but that was a normal reality at events—random interruptions and distractions. I remember one time when she got recognized at a bar while sitting facing the wall. That's how memorable she was. A word comes to mind: *magnetic*.

Educator, welder, fabricator, land-speed record holder, motorcycle builder, TV host, off-road racer, Queen of the Hammers, beautiful badass, intelligent woman.

Rest in peace, Miss Jessi Combs. You changed my life. And I know I'm not the only one who can say that.

The fastest woman on Earth—with a top speed of 522.783 mph (averaged) achieved in the North American Eagle jet car in the Alvord Desert of Oregon. Jessi worked toward her land-speed goal for years. She wanted to top the record of 512.710 mph set in 1976 by Kitty O'Neil, a woman who inspired Jessi for years. When Jessi talked about this project, she'd get light on her feet with stars in her eyes.

She made history in more ways than one when she went for the record in August 2019. She became the fastest woman on Earth after two passes. On her third pass, something went wrong and the North American Eagle crashed. The world lost a legendary woman who stole hearts and inspired millions via television shows like MythBusters, All Girls Garage, and Overhaulin'. Jessi was the first Queen of the Hammers, the first female grand marshal of Sturgis, the original Real Deal woman.

Afterward no one knew if her two passes would be averaged and qualified for the record. The weeks dragged on and months later it was finally announced: Jessi Combs was the fastest woman on Earth. The automotive and motorcycle world rejoiced—Jessi had achieved her goal and raised the bar for future women (and men) who will no doubt be inspired by her achievements.

Jessi Combs lives on in more ways than one. Her mission to get more women into the trades is carried on by the Jessi Combs Foundation and the Real Deal nonprofit she started with Theresa Contreras. The JCF's mission is to "educate, inspire and empower the next generation of female trailblazers & stereotype-breakers." Already the JCF has awarded seven scholarships totaling $30,000 to women pursuing trade work. The Real Deal also works to give people a taste of what it feels like to get your hands dirty and wanting to learn more about welding, pinstriping, blacksmithing, leathercraft, and more.

GLORIA TRAMONTIN STRUCK

INSPIRATION. THIS IS THE WORD THAT COMES TO mind when trying to describe the feeling that Gloria Tramontin Struck sparks. Now in her mid-nineties, Gloria is one of the original matriarchs of modern motorcycling. One of the first Motor Maids, she's clocked over 700,000 miles in her lifetime, and she's never let societal norms dictate her choices.

Started in 1940 with fifty-one charter members, Motor Maids was one of the first women's motorcycling groups. Considered the oldest women's club in the United States, the organization is still rolling with over 1,300 members across North America. Imagining this group of groundbreaking women coming together in the 1940s on loud, rattling, heavy motorcycles is an incredible and goose bump–inducing thought. Seeing a gaggle of ladies rolling down the road on two wheels

is a spectacle today, but it's nearly impossible to imagine eighty years ago. "It wasn't really proper in 1941 for a woman to be riding a motorcycle," Gloria explains. "I have been refused gas and a room and called names. Today, guys *want* their wives or girlfriends to ride. There's no stigma against women riding."

Gloria's love of motorcycling grew over time, but her love of travel was instantaneous. Having owned more than fourteen motorcycles and ridden the lower forty-eight United States multiple times, she yearned for distant continents. Nearly fifty years after first dreaming of riding across Europe, she realized at age seventy-four that she better make it happen. So she and her son Glenn took their bikes to Europe and headed to the Alps. Twenty years later, at age ninety-four, Gloria is still going.

LINDA DUGEAU

BORN IN MASSACHUSETTS IN 1913, LINDA DUGEAU learned to ride on her (future) husband Bud's Harley-Davidson when she was nineteen. "The minute I saw it I wanted to ride," she said. She quickly fell in love and became an ardent motorcyclist devoted to bringing women riders together. Her adventures were featured in the pages of *Motorcyclist* magazine, and she later became a dispatch rider.

Dot Robinson, an Australian born in 1912, and Linda became close friends and accomplices in their mission for connecting lady riders. Dot, who moved to the United States in 1918 because of her father's expanding sidecar business, was both a lady and a fierce competitor. Attempts to prevent her from competing in endurance runs impassioned her to empower other women. Telling strong women what they can and cannot do has often been the catalyst for great change, and this was one of those times.

In 1938 Linda and Dot set in motion the events that created America's first women's motorcycle

DOT ROBINSON

club. It wasn't easy. First Linda wrote letter after letter to dealers, riders, AMA members, and others. Dot went on a cross-country road trip, contacting women who owned and rode their own motorcycles. Almost three years later, in 1930, the pair were joined by thirty-nine other women for a meeting of minds and motorcycles. They settled on the name "Motor Maids" and created their bylaws. They wanted to be taken seriously, and they wanted to get somewhere. The club was modeled after the Ninety-Nines (Amelia Earhart's organization for women pilots) and had two rules: (1) a Motor Maid must own her own motorcycle, and (2) she must at all times conduct herself like a lady.

Although Linda and Dot are no longer with us, Motor Maids now has over 1,300 members around the world. Both of these wonderful women can also be found in the AMA Hall of Fame . . . and in many of our hearts.

VALERIE THOMPSON

THE FASTEST WOMAN ON TWO WHEELS . . . what a title. Valerie Thompson is a fearless badass operating in a field dominated by graybeards with petrol in their veins and salt under their fingernails. Her top speed is a bone rattling 328 miles per hour, one of her eight land-speed records. She is a member of seven 200-miles-per-hour clubs, one 300-miles-per-hour club, and the Sturgis Motorcycle Hall of Fame.

Born in Tacoma, Washington, Thompson always had a flair for going fast. After high school, she got a little '64 Volkswagen Beetle and customized it to show quality. "On the street people always wanted to race me, and I'd yell, 'Come on, Betsy, let's go!'" she recalls. Her love of motorcycles came later. Having no family or friends involved in riding, she didn't get on a bike until age thirty-two. After she took some scoots on the back of a friend's motorcycle, he suddenly stopped wanting her as a passenger because her jeans scratched his fender. When he suggested she buy her own bike,

off to the dealership they went. "That's what created a little monster in me," she says with a laugh. Valerie's first bike was a Sportster 1200 that lasted only three months before getting traded in for something bigger to keep up with her riding buddies: a Harley-Davidson Fat Boy.

Thompson's grandparents heavily encouraged her to pursue a career in banking, just as her aunt—who was like a second mom to Thompson—had done. "I was a little peon, and I worked all the way up to the legal department," Thompson recalls, "and then I got laid off." She took her severance and moved on, shedding her dresses for biker clothes in a transformative experience.

By that time, most of her friends were motorcyclists. She credits a lot of the riding skills she's used throughout her racing career to their time on the road together, traveling to events like the Four Corners Rally, Daytona Bike Week, and Sturgis. After

attending Arizona Bike Week, Thompson fell in love with the state and didn't want to leave. After moving there in 2004, she met a new group of riding buddies, one of whom told her she needed to take her speed racer mentality to the track. So Charlie Mitchell and Thompson headed to the races. "I didn't know what I was doing and neither did he," she says. "It was just one of those fun things. It kind of inspired me to be a better rider and a better racer." The fastest woman on two wheels, and it all began on a quarter-mile drag strip. "Bad things happen when you're not in control, so taking it to the track was the best decision I could've made," she says. "That started my career." Her competitive nature drove her to become better, and she attended George Bryce's Pro Stock Motorcycle School in Florida four times.

Thompson's fiery desire to be better and faster inspires her to achieve the amazing speeds she does. She doesn't have a role model from racing or otherwise, and for the longest time denied being one herself. "I didn't sign up to be an inspiration," she insists. "I guess I had something in me that I was doing, and everyone liked that." She's incredibly unpretentious about being on posters that hang on garage walls around the world. These days she's excited to share what she does. "I'm just thankful to have motorcycles as a platform and that I am an inspiration to both men and women. Now I get to use my racing to inspire people. My success is a payoff to help others."

Despite many triumphs and speed records in the past fifteen years, lately it's not been the smoothest track. A crash in 2018 and shutdowns from the COVID-19 pandemic didn't douse her plans, though. "I feel like a bottle of wine, I just age gracefully and get faster and faster," says Thompson, who plans to add Fastest Driver in a Piston-Engined Car to her list of accolades by attempting 500-plus miles per hour on four wheels.

HANNAH JOHNSON

HANNAH JOHNSON IS A FIERY PERSONALITY AND, most notably in the world of two wheels, the first female Ducati master technician. Let me repeat that: Hannah Johnson was the first woman on planet Earth to earn the master technician certification at Ducati. She is fast as hell, and she helped me tear down my Ducati Monster that turned into the semifamous build named "Pandora's Box." Sometimes all it takes is someone else connecting with you and having faith in your abilities to give you the motivation to work on things yourself and take mechanical matters into your own hands.

In motorcycling our first feeling isn't "Do I belong here?" but instead "I want to find my people."

Hannah did that. She worked at Ducati Miami for five years, ending with title service manager before eventually moving to Portland, Oregon, to work for MotoCorsa in the same capacity.

In her years in the motorcycle industry, Hannah has smashed through the ceiling, paving the way for other women motorcyclists. She was the only woman in her technician classes. Today in America, about 14 percent of motorcyclists are women. While the intricate pieces of Ducati engines might benefit from a feminine touch, it seems that all of motorcycling is benefiting similarly. Hannah has been a large part of that movement.

LESLIE PORTERFIELD IS ANOTHER ONE OF OUR amazingly fast moto ladies. Holding the Guinness World Record for Fastest Woman on a Conventional Motorcycle (in other words, not a streamliner like Valerie Thompson pilots), she averaged 232.522 mph at the Bonneville Salt Flats in 2008. She was also the first woman on a motorcycle inducted into the Bonneville 200 MPH Club, breaking a sixty-one-year streak.

When first getting into riding at sixteen years old, Leslie took to the salt flat land-speed racing scene in 2007 at the BUB Motorcycle Speed Trials. Her goals were thwarted by a 110-mph crash that ended in a punctured lung, seven broken ribs, a concussion, and a helicopter ride. Despite all that, she was back in the saddle in 2008 on her 2000cc turbocharged Suzuki Hayabusa for a second attempt at breaking Marcia Holley's thirty-year-old speed record of 229.361 mph. On September 5, 2008, her two opposing-direction mile-long runs averaged a speed of 232.522 mph. Later that year she was honored as the AMA's 2008 Female Rider of the Year.

"I don't just want to be the fastest woman in the world," she says. "I want to be the fastest person in the world. That's what's next."

THIS INCREDIBLE WOMAN, LAIA SANZ PLA-GIRIBERT, was born in Barcelona, Spain. One of the lucky ones to start young, Laia rode her first bike with her dad at just two years old. She was encouraged to race by her mom for the first time in 1992, at a Catalan Championship race for kids in her hometown, Corbera de Llobregat. Although she finished in the bottom of the group in eighth place, the spark turned to a flame.

In 1997, Laia participated in her first female trials championship with fifty other girls from around the world and also took her first victory in a male category

on an 80cc trial bike. She was only twelve years old. But it was in 2001 when she really found her place on the podiums, winning the Women's Trial World Championship and securing second place at the European version. Since then she's become a thirteen-time Women's World Trial champion and ten-time Trial European champion, has taken home the women's motorbike trophy at Rally Dakar seven times, and is a six-time winner at the Women's Trial des Nations.

KATE JOHNSTON

EVER HEARD OF AN IRON BUTT RIDE? WELL, there's actually an association that dictates what exactly one of these events must comprise. There are rules and subtypes of rides, including "Bun Burner," "SaddleSore," . . . well, you get the idea. One of the most challenging is the "Ultimate Coast to Coast to Coast Insanity Ride," which Kate Johnston completed on a BMW f700GS.

Many riders don't venture into ultra-long distance riding, especially when starting out. Kate had only been riding three years when she took off to complete the long-distance ride. The Ultimate Coast to Coast to Coast Insanity Ride challenges riders to make it from one coast to the other in under sixty days—and then turn around and do the same the other way. To qualify for this Iron Butt, the rider must have completed one of the following: a Bun Burner Gold, SaddleSore 2000, Alberta 2000, Capitol 1000, Nevada 1100, Minnesota 1000, TimberButt, Tarbutt Rally, Utah 1088, any Cognoscente Group event, any Reno BMW long-distance event, any Motorcycle Endurance Rider Association (MERA) event, or the Iron Butt Rally.

A total of 13,560 miles for the whole trip, and 10,767 miles of those were in twenty-four days for the CCC Insanity ride.

Kate is the first woman in history to have completed this trip as the motorcycle operator rather than passenger. And it wasn't easy. Temperatures ranged from 101°F in Tennessee to snow flurries and 40°F in Alaska. Kate and her bike both took a beating when it rained on three of her four days on the Dalton Highway. Being a diabetic, she has to pay proper attention to her diet and carry medical supplies. This is something most of us take for granted on long trips—when was the last time you ate right while you were on a long road trip? These weren't the only tough parts of the trip, though one of the scariest had to be on her first day riding the remote Dalton Highway when she saw a wolf alongside

the road as she approached. Kate thought that it would run off; instead, it ran straight at her. Horsepower over paws, she gassed it and sailed safely past.

So why did she do it? "I wanted an adventure," she explains. "You read and see all these people going on grand adventures. I wanted to go on a great adventure. It just happened that I was the first woman to do that, but that was like a little cherry on the cake."

So would she recommend such a road trip to others? "I think everyone should take a trip by themselves at some point. You get to know yourself when all the things that revolve around us in life disappear." Well said.

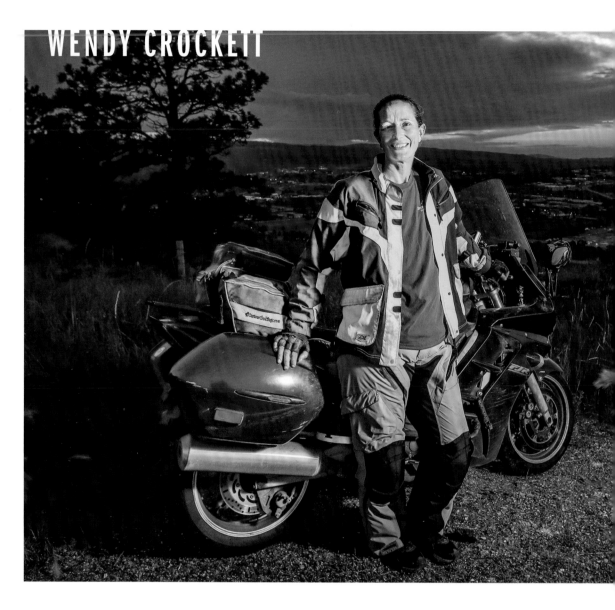

MOTORCYCLE MECHANIC WENDY CROCKETT was the first-ever woman to win an Iron Butt Rally, completing 13,000 miles in eleven days in 2019. To be exact, she rode 12,998.9 miles, scoring 154,086 points—the second-highest mileage score in Iron Butt history. She explained that her motivation didn't come from a desire to beat others but wanting to compete against herself.

In her words, the Iron Butt Rally is "basically a nationwide scavenger hunt." First held in 1984 and becoming "official" in 1991, the rally takes place every other year and lasts a total of eleven days with a base total of 11,000 miles. Riders are given a rally pack that includes checkpoints and bonus locations. Riders must arrive at various checkpoints by given times to be counted, and bonus locations include challenges for extra points. There are over 75,000 Iron Butt Association members across the United States, often called the "World's Toughest Riders." In recent years, these events have had around seventy

finishing riders, and Wendy's scores have been among the best of the best.

No stranger to hard work, Wendy became a certified motorcycle mechanic after attending the Motorcycle Mechanics Institute (MMI) for two and a half years. Since then she's run a successful motorcycle shop in California, completed multiple endurance rallies, and took second place in the Ten 'N Ten Rally (10,000 miles in ten days) twice in a row. Her two-wheel travels aren't limited to rallies and competitions—she's also ridden the corners of North America and explored Mexico and Newfoundland, Key West and the Arctic Circle.

JENNY TINMOUTH

JENNY TINMOUTH IS THE WORLD'S FASTEST woman around the Isle of Man TT, the first and only female to compete in the British Superbike Championship, and the first woman to win a British Supersport Championship race. She holds two Guinness World Records for the previously mentioned achievements. Pretty amazing!

At thirty-six years old, when most racers would be retiring, she was announced as the third Honda Racer for British Superbike racing, joining Jason O'Halloran and Dan Linfoot on the factory Honda CBR1000RR in 2015. Tinmouth admitted she was surprised to be approached. "I'm absolutely over the Moon and cannot believe I'm riding for Honda Racing in the British Superbike Championship," she says. "The offer was totally unexpected. I went into the meeting thinking it would just be some help and came out as a full-time Honda rider. It's always been my ultimate dream to ride for the team."

On top of achieving her dream as a rider for Honda Racing, her racing history is nothing short of incredible. She earned her first Guinness World

Record in 2009 during her first-ever Isle of Man TT race, returning in June 2010 to break her own record for fastest ever lap by a woman on the 37.73-mile course: 18:52.42 at an average speed of 119.945 mph. Mind you, this is known as the world's most dangerous race, and even in the professional world of motorbike racing is not at all for the faint of heart.

In what was technically her third Guinness record, Jenny became the first woman to compete in the British Superbike Championship in 2011 on an Aprilia RSV4 1000. At the International Visionary Awards, she was given the "It Girl" award by the Women's International Film and Television Showcase for her dedication in her sport and its far-reaching inspiration.

BERYL SWAIN

"WOMEN, THE WEAKER SEX, ARE MUSCLING IN on man's domain, practically no sport is sacred." Ahh, that old 1960s attitude. This is what one reporter wrote about Beryl Swain, trailblazing Isle of Man TT racer who wound up banned from the event for being a woman. Often called the "First Lady" of the TT, Beryl entered the Ultra Lightweight class in 1962 when she was twenty-six years old, becoming the race's first solo female competitor.

In the early '50s, Beryl was working at a shipping company as a secretary. She fell in love with Eddie Swain, a racer who ran his own shop, and the two married seven years later. Beryl was hands-on with Eddie's race bikes, helping prep for events across England and eventually itching to race herself. Soon enough she was twisting the throttle on track, trying 500cc motorcycles but favoring smaller 50cc bikes and nearly breaking a little-bike record at Brands Hatch. "This was my first try for six months and my hands were frozen 'round the twistgrip," she related to a newspaper, "but I was told I had managed to get within three seconds of the lap record for 50ccs."

The Isle of Man TT, even to this day known as the most dangerous race on Earth, is an intimidating course around the island and nearly 38 miles in length. Varying from sea level to 1,300-foot elevation, the

course has a wild array of challenging features like tight turns through town streets. Gearing up for the race, Beryl took it upon herself to get press for the event. "I have been doing all I can to give lady riders as much publicity as possible," she said. Two of Beryl's close friends, who were also riders and racers, Pat Wise and Margo Pearson, had considered taking part in the Isle of Man TT race. Pat wasn't able to secure an international racing license, however, and Margo waffled on the idea.

This time it was Beryl's hubby's turn to prep *her* bike, and he got the rare Italian 50cc Itom. She finished twenty-second of twenty-five and was ecstatic to return the following year. However the FIM had different ideas and revoked her racing license because, basically, they felt the death of a female rider in the Isle of Man TT would be bad press. (Since the first race in 1907, there have been 151 deaths on the official racecourse.) Despite an outpouring of support from fans, fellow racers, and the lieutenant governor of the Isle of Man, the FIM would not budge. Another woman would not ride the course until 1978.

Beryl hung up her leathers and went to work managing multiple London locations of a grocery chain. Though she did not race again, her accomplishments were featured prominently in an exhibit called "Fast Women" at the Manx Museum in Douglas, Isle of Man.

Not many motorcyclists can say they've held a Guinness World Record. Likewise few have met the Royal Family. Maria Costello is the only female motorcycle racer to have ever received the title of Member of the Order of the British Empire (MBE). Her countless other awards range from the East Midlands Racing Association (EMRA) Best Lady to the Fastest Woman Ever at Manx Grand Prix in 2002. In 2010 she became the fastest woman to lap the Ulster Grand Prix. Covering each of her achievements and races would take pages and pages. Now in her forties, Maria still races professionally.

Despite a terrible crash at the Isle of Man TT in 1999, Maria returned to compete in the race in 2002. Just two years later, in 2004, she secured the Guinness World Record as the fastest woman to lap the course with an average speed of 114.73 mph. She held this record for six years before Jenny Tinmouth set a new

record in 2009. No stranger to making history, Maria is still the first and only female solo racer to have taken the podium at the Isle of Man Grand Prix.

Competing alongside the guys for most of her life, Maria isn't easily deterred. Having broken twenty-four bones during her racing career, she keeps going because the rewards are worth the risks. "Racing motorbikes is the best thing I've ever done," she says. "It has its up and downs, and I've broken over twenty bones, but I've not found anything that gives me the same buzz to replace it."

Her ambition and determination have made her a success on and off the racetrack. She's a published author, member of the Fédération Internationale de Motocyclisme (FIM) Women in Motorcycling Commission, 2005 BBC Sports Personality of the Year, a character in a PlayStation Game, and, most notably, a force to be reckoned with whether on two wheels or two feet.

MARY MCGEE IS A PIONEER IN AMERICAN motorcycle racing, thanks to her untamable determination and a spirit as warm as her smile. Her excitement for motorcycling, especially racing, is contagious even in her eighties. She was the first woman to receive an FIM racing license in the United States and to race the Baja 500 solo. She was also inducted into the AMA Hall of Fame.

Born in Juneau, Alaska, in 1936, Mary and her family relocated to Phoenix, Arizona, in 1944 because of the threat of Japanese attack during World War II. At twenty she married a skilled race car mechanic who would introduce her to the rubber-burning world of road racing. Shortly after their wedding, she hopped in the driver's seat and started racing with the best of 'em. Donning a pink polka dot helmet in her Sports Car Club of America (SCCA) races, she showed up the boys from inside Ferraris, Porsches, and Jaguars, winning race after race. Soon after she picked up a friend's 200cc Triumph Tiger Cub, and a fire was breathed to life.

Getting into motorcycle racing posed its own set of challenges. Despite her successes on four wheels, the American Federation of Motorcyclists (AFM) needed more reassurance of her skills in the saddle. After passing her skills test she became the first woman to earn an FIM racing license from the AFM in the States. This led to many historical moments for Mary. In a 1962 *Motor Trend* article titled "Housewives Revolt!" the author wrote, "So ladies, if your life is dull and you are bored with freeway traffic, don't give up. Buy a motorcycle and join Mary McGee."

Mary's life seems nothing short of movie worthy when you learn how she got the idea to pick up off-road racing. A year after her feature in *Motor Trend*, she attended a New Year's Eve party where the one and only Steve McQueen gave her a friendly hard time. "McGee, you've got to get off that pansy road-racing bike and come out to the desert," he said. So she did! In 1975, equipped with a 205cc Husqvarna and an unshakeable will, she finished the Baja 500. "I did it, I finished. I think I was seventeenth," she recalls. Her solo finish beat almost twenty two-man teams.

Racing in the Baja 500 is no easy feat even in the modern day, but in 1975 it came with a whole other set of challenges. Today there is still a whole lot of nothing out in the desert, but back then there was no electricity, no doctors, no phones. "I carried Percodan in case of injury," she said, "because you'd have to ride injured to get to someplace where someone has a car to get to Ensenada or La Paz or to a clinic or back to the States." She said though she never had to use the painkillers, she did come off the bike more than once.

McGee has described herself as "fast on my feet, fast with my brain, self-conscious, and lacking confidence," but she had "no trouble with confidence on the racetrack." It's another example of how motorcycling and following your passion can boost personal growth and inspire others to find their happy place.

Mary's AMA Hall of Fame nomination letter said it well: "Her genuine love of people and her ability to communicate her love of motorcycling to others has won her fans throughout the world."

As Mary puts it, "Motorcycling equals freedom, plus it's such fun."

ANA CARRASCO GABARRÓN

A WOMAN WHO HOLDS MANY FIRSTS IN RACING history, Spanish road racer Ana Carrasco Gabarrón was born in 1997 and started her two-wheel career only three years later. Her father Alfonso, an expert motorcycle mechanic who worked with MotoGP racing legend José David de Gea, picked up a minibike for her five-year-old sister, who took little interest in the machine. By four years old Ana was officially competing, and by nine was racing 70cc minibikes and was dubbed "Rider of the Year" by the Spanish company Planet Moto.

Ana continued to compete in amateur and junior categories, taking home victories in two 125cc championships in 2009. Fast forward a few short years and in 2011 she entered the FIM CEV International Championship, where she became the first women to score points in the series. In 2013 she moved on to the more well-known Moto3 World Championship, where she really started to find traction. Repeating her earlier move, she became the first female to score points in this series as well.

Years went on and Ana continued to improve her racing skills and position on the scoreboards. During the Supersport 300 World Championship's debut year in 2017, Ana became the first female to win a single stage of a world championship moto race with an exciting move, overtaking two riders on the final lap at the Algarve International Circuit in Portugal. She found her groove, going on to achieve her best "first" yet: the first woman to win a road-racing world championship

in 2018, making history and headlines around the globe when she was just twenty-two years old.

When asked about racing with all the guys, she recalls, "The first year was really difficult; the riders were not ready to have a woman on the grid." While they didn't say anything to her directly, she could feel it. "You could just tell what they thought. They didn't want to look at me and I had to do everything alone." While other riders usually find a mentor in an older rider, she was left to her own devices. "I had to learn how to be fast alone."

On top of being a woman in a male-dominated sport, Ana isn't exactly formidable in physical stature. At just over 5-foot-1, she's a testament to the fact that physical size has nothing to do with the ability

to operate a motorcycle. In fact, if you can get comfortable with feeling a little *short* in the inseam region, being smaller can come with advantages. Hell, people spend countless dollars every year to shave weight off their vehicles.

While racing is undeniably one of her passions, Ana is also pursuing a law degree. Perhaps her cleverness fueled her decision to have her own umbrella boy on the grid at the 2014 Assen Dutch TT. "I was happy. I said: 'They have grid girls, why can't I have a grid guy?'" she recalls. "So for one race it happened and we showed people women don't just have to be grid girls. They can race too."

46

Taru Rinne was born in Turku, Finland, in 1968. Early in her foray into racing she was primarily rocking karts, winning the Finnish Karting Championship (85cc class) in 1979. Racing against future Formula One drivers like Mika Häkkinen, Mika Salo, and Jyrki Järvilehto, she often beat them out, including at the Karting Championship in 1979 and again in 1982.

Taru changed gears to motorcycles and became the first woman to get points in MotoGP when she started in 1988. In 1989 she qualified second in the 125cc class at Hockenheim. Taru eventually stopped racing when she received a letter from Bernie Ecclestone, who was in charge of deciding riders' fates on the track. Ecclestone disqualified her from the following racing season after a crash.

Taru is still a legend in women's motorcycle racing, remaining a proud proponent of fast women.

ADVENTURERS

"WOMAN CAN, IF SHE WILL." –AUGUSTA VAN BUREN, 1916

In a world of nine-to-five jobs filled with cubicles that can drain the essence of one's being, the average person finds a way to be content with weekend adventures and (maybe) yearly vacations.

That reality couldn't be further from the truth for these women riders. Instead of jobs being the vehicle by which they make their living, their vehicle is the way they live. Their jobs often last just as long as necessary to make the money needed to escape "normal" life, to chase those fleeting moments of perfection—beautiful vistas glowing at sunset, sights that seem almost too picturesque to be anything but an oil painting, meeting people in the middle of nowhere with stories that blow your mind.

The allure of life on the road is strong enough for these women to ignore language barriers and the inherent dangers of solo travel. The magic of crunching miles beneath their wheels drives them to undertake massive road trips, racking up tens of thousands of miles across continents and even around the world. The tribulations are often as many as the triumphs, but you can't have adventure if everything goes smoothly. Travelers must have the ability to roll with the punches, to adapt and compromise, to be open to all types of new experiences . . .

One thing is certain, all these ladies have shown incredible will, courage, and the ability to adapt.

LOIS PRYCE

BRITISH AUTHOR LOIS PRYCE IS ONE OF THE best-known women in the realm of adventure riding, and for good reason. Many of her trips have been groundbreaking, and she's written three books about her journeys. Not only is she an indomitable adventurer, having taken off on solo tours of Iran, the Americas, and Africa, but she's also a sailing enthusiast, a banjo player in an all-female bluegrass band called the Jolenes, and a writer whose byline has appeared in *The Independent, The Guardian, The Telegraph,* and CNN. She's also the great-granddaughter of Nobel-winning physicist Max Born and closely related to singer and actress Olivia Newton-John.

Now in her forties, Lois got her motorcycle license at twenty-nine while living in London. As a product manager for BBC Music, she found herself with restless wheel syndrome. When Bob the Builder topped the singles chart, she knew she had to ditch her cubicle job for the open road.

As a woman, riding a motorcycle can be a daunting task in and of itself, whether it's the anxiety of walking into a motorcycle shop full of guys or the frustration of finding someone to help you learn about the mechanical workings of your bike without talking to you like you're an idiot because you weren't born with a wrench in your hand. Even when riding around, you sometimes hear comments so stupid you can barely believe it. "Hey, need me to show you how to ride that thing?" or "Oh, cool bike. Whose is it?"

While all her trips are amazing in their own way, two stand out for their possible ramifications in modern world climates—or just for Lois's straight-up ballsiness for diving right into the deep end. In 2003 she hit the road on a Yamaha XT225, riding 20,000 miles from Alaska to the southernmost tip of Argentina, Ushuaia. But perhaps most shocking to hear these days is that she took a two-month solo trip across Iran that helped dispel some of the common misconceptions about the Iranian people and Islam. When Lois ventured alone

into Iran, the Foreign Office strongly suggested against visiting under any circumstances, warning, "British nationals could be detained in Iran despite their complete innocence."

She went anyway, with only herself, essentials packed tightly in her luggage, and her trusty motorbike. "On the one hand I'd hear awful things about women being stoned for adultery, the highest rate of execution in the world, and nuclear enriching," she says. "Then overland travelers would say Iran was wonderful and their favorite country. That difference intrigued me. I was aware that there was an element of risk, as there is no British representation in Iran, but I believed that it was a risk worth taking—and I am so glad I did."

Lois admits that she set off on the trip with a certain level of trepidation. "Was it really wise for me to ride a motorcycle alone in this pariah nation of Islamic extremists, with all its gruesome facts and figures surrounding women's rights, free speech, and treatment of political prisoners?" she wonders. But she isn't one to be swayed by popular opinions conveyed through media and governments. "If I've learned anything from my travels, it's that a nation's government and its people are entirely unconnected."

Lois says her travels through Iran were some of the most profoundly enriching of all her journeys. At times she was pushed off the road by vehicles, but not out of malice—rather, to give her gifts like bags of pomegranates. Iranian culture, she discovered, is one of great hospitality, unparalleled by any she'd experienced before.

Lois's willingness to swim against the current in her professional endeavors and her travels is a shining example for all of us, a lesson to not allow fear, self-doubt, and external influences to get in our way. The only voice that matters is your own, the one that tells you to get on the road and find what you're looking for.

ADELINE & AUGUSTA VAN BUREN

IN THE SUMMER OF 1916, TWO FEARLESS sisters decided to assert their independence by embarking on a cross-country solo motorcycle adventure. Though women still could not vote in the United States, nor were they allowed in the military, Adeline and Augusta Van Buren were chomping at the bit to prove that women were more than capable of serving as dispatch riders in the U.S. military.

Addie and Gussie, as family and friends called them, were born in 1884 and 1889, respectively, into a cushy life as descendants of eighth president Martin Van Buren. They acquired two well-equipped Indian Powerplus motorcycles for their trek. These top-of-the-line models went for $275 at the time and were the same bikes used in the military.

Unlike their upbringing, the excursion would be anything but cushy. Their bikes may have had "nonskid" Bridgestone tires and the best headlights on the market, but nothing could prepare them for the road, or lack thereof, ahead. The idea was to take the Lincoln Highway, a road running from New York City to San Francisco. Reality proved more difficult than expected, however, with the "highway," it turned out, comprising wagon trails, cow passes, and the like.

Out in the thick of it, Addie and Gussie found themselves battling incredible obstacles. They were arrested in small towns outside Chicago for wearing men's clothes (their protective leathers). West of the Mississippi, their course was repeatedly swept away by rains and wind.

In August, already far behind schedule, the sisters became the first women to summit 14,109-foot Pikes Peak in Colorado, still facing many more weeks of arduous travel. In the Rocky Mountains storms left

them battling trails that sucked their tires deep into the mire and stranded the pair in freezing conditions miles from help. They set off on foot in the darkness and hours later found themselves in a small mining town where the fellas were more than happy to help two trailblazing women on an epic pilgrimage. In the desert outside of Salt Lake City the sisters were again lost, stranded, and almost out of water. Again locals came to their aid.

Adeline and Augusta rolled into San Francisco on September 2. Sadly their endeavor was touted by the media as a ladies' vacation, with focus put on their machines rather than their indomitable spirit. And although their subsequent applications to the military dispatch service were rejected, history will never forget them as the first women to complete a cross-country motorcycle journey. In 2002 they were inducted into the AMA Motorcycle Hall of Fame for their incredible history-making road trip.

ALICIA SORNOSA

A BIT OF A DAREDEVIL, ALICIA SORNOSA LIKES things that'll give her a thrill—from snowboarding and sailing to anything with an engine. In 2011 she hopped in the saddle for a round-the-world tour and hasn't stopped rolling since. She's the first Spanish woman to complete such a trip, having ridden five continents and more than fifty-one countries. In 2016 she published her first novel, *360 Grados*, based on her trip around the world. As of early 2020, she had clocked more than 177,000 miles and was still on the move!

Alicia began her travels on a BMW F650GS (which, in the world of adventure motorcycles, is on the not-huge side) equipped with loads of luggage and spare tires. Crossing oceans and riding uncharted territories on such a seemingly cumbersome machine worried her loved ones, but Alicia (who stands just over 5 feet tall) persisted to Africa and beyond. When you roam because you can't stand sitting still—when watching the world pass by is decidedly not in your nature—traveling is as restorative as it is risky. But just as there are no rainbows without rain, you can't get to the most beautiful sights without hitting some dirt.

While Alicia's many exploits have yielded personal rewards, her endeavors on two wheels often have a charitable element as well. A recent trip riding through Nepal and India, for example, allowed her to raise money for people affected by the 2015 Earthquake that devastated the region. She also uses her journalism skills and leverages social media to promote causes like building wells in Ethiopia with the NGO (nongovernmental organization) Amigos de Silva. Wherever she travels, Alicia works with an NGO to help make a difference in the world she is visiting. It's an example we can all learn from.

INDIAN SOLO MOTO TRAVELER ESHA GUPTA found her way to motorcycles through adventure rather than the other way around. As a backpacker, she met a group of bikers in Ladakh who inspired her to look into motorbikes as a mode of travel and an appealing alternative to the region's often packed buses. In 2011, she quit her corporate job and decided to roam full time, leading to her first two-wheeled solo expedition: completing the Golden Quadrilateral, more than 3,700 miles of national highways connecting the four major cities of India—all from behind the bars of her Bajaj Avenger named "Mike." Yep . . . Mike the Bike.

India at the time was raw and in an uproar after a 2012 gang rape and murder in South Delhi led to great concern about women's safety. Naturally such a tragedy had significant effects. People looked over their shoulders more, hugged their loved ones a little tighter. Some decided not to go on that road trip with their friends. Esha, however, wanted to show that her country was indeed safe. "All the brouhaha on social media had tarnished the country's image and I wanted to send a message that was contrary to everybody's belief," she recalls. "Today, I can definitely say India is not so bad a country for women."

Esha is no stranger to iron-butt endurance riding, either. She holds records in Asia, India, and the *Golden Book of World Records* for the Longest Journey on a Bike in a Single Country by a Woman. It may not be the longest ever, but it's impressive nonetheless. Esha completed just under 20,000 miles (32,187 kilometers over there) through sixteen Indian states in 110 days—nearly 280 miles a day. Throughout all of this, her objective was to highlight the positive aspects of her country, sharing her experiences at every possible opportunity. During a nasty cyclone in the ancient temple-rich eastern state of Odisha

(formerly Orissa), a young man led her through the mess. "I blindly followed him for over ten kilometers through a deserted area at the end of which, after dropping at the nearest town, he called me *didi*," she says (the term means "older sister"). "Good people are everywhere. My experience of trusting people has never gone wrong."

SHERRI JO WILKINS

BECAUSE I CAN! HAVE YOU EVER WANTED TO scream that at the top of your lungs? Maybe not since you were a kid, but somewhere deep down you've felt it as an adult too. Sherri Jo Wilkins flaunted her choice to do what she damn well pleases when she hit the road for a three-and-a-half-year round-the-world trip in 2010. The tour took Sherri Jo through forty-nine countries over an impressive 86,000 miles.

One thing about women motorcycle adventurers seems true across the board: they have a penchant for excitement that most would consider dangerous. Sherri Jo is no different and lived a colorful life even before hopping on two wheels for her great trek, from rocking the copilot seat as a navigator in light aircraft to dodging pirates while sailing through Pacific isles. Originally from Indianapolis, Indiana, she was an avid Harley rider who got her start on motorcycles on the back of her dad's Goldwing. After moving to Australia and learning to sail, the adventure bug continued to gnaw. That's where the seed for the "Because I Can World Tour" was planted.

In preparation for her big trip, she needed the right bike for the job. The search for a BMW adventure bike began. While on her way back to the dealership from her F800GS test ride, she dumped the bike in an intersection, damaging the turn signal and giving it some fresh scrapes. She was alone and could have kept the little fumble to herself. Instead she wrote about it and shared it with the world. In a culture where we're all using apps to filter our faces and preening ourselves for our social media pages, this honesty is a commendable and inspiring notion. Referring to an award-winning sailor on her blog, Sherri Jo wrote, "It's not the end of the world, and I just remembered that young Jessica Watson crashed her yacht into a cargo ship on her test run."

This kind of attitude is undoubtedly a huge part of Sherri Jo's success, especially on two wheels.

AILEEN GUENTHER

In 2014 German-born Aileen Guenther was gearing up for a round-the-world adventure. As she built her scrambler from the ground up, striking photos featuring a redhead wielding a blowtorch over a little bike stripped down to the chassis made the rounds on web platforms. Women's solo moto travel still isn't the most normal thing—and it's even rarer for the bike to be built by the rider. Aileen's out-of-the-box approach to travel—rad custom Honda Tiger 200, bright smile, sunny personality—all made her "Moto Quest" an especially exciting trip to tune into.

Aileen wanted to make it known that Moto Quest would *not* be just another travel, lifestyle, or motorcycle blog. The intention wasn't to highlight destinations, motorcycles, or the creature comforts of a simpler, "elevated" way of living. Instead she wrote about broadening her horizons, and of the transformation and healing guided by her spirit, heart, and intuition.

Practically synonymous with freedom, the motorcycle was a perfect vehicle for that exploration and growth. Admittedly past experiences riding Australia's blacktop on a café racer Honda CD250U (her sole transportation for two years) only *sort of* prepared her for the road ahead. "I've chosen to try and break the mold. To champion my own destiny and set out for a big adventure," Aileen explained. "I'm saddling up for an arduous metamorphosis."

Aileen's big quest wasn't fueled simply by curiosity or travel lust, surely good enough reasons all on their own. After living for more than four years in Melbourne, she was unable to renew her Australian visa and had to move. She was forced to leave her friends, partner, and home behind at age twenty-nine. To top it off, doctors cautioned her that the ongoing health condition she'd been suffering from since childhood was incurable. Told she may never

make it to thirty, she promised herself to create a life worth waking up to every morning.

After having times in her life when walking ten steps was an ordeal, she approached Moto Quest as another challenge she would face with grace. "There's a health aspect of this journey that makes it almost impossible—that's why I'm doing it," Aileen wrote. "Because I don't know if I can. I want to experience the ability of my spirit to overcome physical boundaries and what others say cannot be done. I am a spirited warrior who gratefully faces every moment and challenge of life with excitement and a positive attitude."

Forced out of her Australian comfort zone, Aileen was thrown back into the saddle and onto the road. Unfortunately due to the visa issues caused by her employer, Aileen recalled, "I ended up in Bali, not knowing what to do with my life." Exiled and trying to

figure out her next move, she chose to make lemonade instead of complaining about sour fruit.

Strong-willed in the best of ways, Aileen plotted, planned, and began work on her motorcycle with the guys at the Verve Moto shop in Bali. The used Honda was closely inspected, tuned, and given a full bars-to-bodywork custom job: tank, fenders, fairing, exhaust, seat, and bars, all tweaked and fabricated for the Moto Quest bike and its pilot. While Aileen's parents always frowned on Aileen getting her hands dirty, she was finally able to fulfill her mechanical fantasies by acquiring the necessary knowledge for a solo trip, from fundamentals like bulb replacements and battery basics to cleaning carbs, checking and adjusting chain tension, patching and plugging tires, and more. She set off on her bike with a load of new knowledge and the attitude needed for any trip into the unknown: a willingness to adapt, enjoy, and be flexible.

EGLĖ GERULAITYTĖ

66

ADVENTURERS ★ EGLĖ GERULAITYTĖ

EGLÉ GERULAITYTÉ IS A WORLD EXPLORER BASED in Lithuania. She has turned her tales of motorcycle travels into successful adventure news sites, writing for BBC Travel, cofounding *Women ADV Riders magazine*, and becoming the senior writer at *ADV Rider* and a contributing writer for *ADV Pulse*. Eglé's informative articles for motorcyclists trying to get into adventure riding or honing their road-trip skills offer a variety of wisdom-laden how-to lists and insights.

Eglé got her first taste of the romance of rally racing while chasing the Dakar Rally in Peru in 2019 in what was her first multiday roadbook navigation challenge. The decision to chase the Dakar was last minute and loosely planned at best. Her travels had taken her to Peru at an opportune time to join in on the dirt-flinging festivities. In order to keep up with the ever-moving riders, lend a helping hand, maintain her own motorcycle, and take photos, she "slept little, covered long distances, endured scorching desert sun, and ran around sleepy Peruvian fishing villages in search [of] spare parts, cold Red Bull, or confused support teams getting lost en route to their hotels." After ten days of crust, dust, and at times dismal conditions, Eglé had lost over 20 pounds, toasted her clutch, and found a new addiction. She described it as "probably the most intense experience of my motorcycling life."

Then in 2019 Eglé took her Suzuki DR650 named "Lucy" straight into the fire, as they say, entering the Hellas Rally in Greece and going for broke in a discipline totally new to her. Part of her preparations included two sessions with rider and coach Mykolas Paulavicius. While not a strenuous amount of training, it helped her get more comfortable and confident in sand, something incredibly helpful for nearly all rally racing. By day five of the race, Eglé had sprained her clutch hand, was getting fatigued, and realized that she lacked confidence and speed in technical areas. But most importantly, she finished and learned something that we can all apply to our two-wheel journeys (and beyond): "Humans are limitless, and nothing is impossible."

STEPH JEAVONS

Steph Jeavons from Colwyn Bay, North Wales, has traveled more in her short time on Earth than most of us will ever dream of. In 2014 she closed her business, sold her stuff, and took off on a round-the-world trip during which she became a grandma.

Steph had given birth to her son at eighteen years old and soon thereafter began dreaming of travel and world adventure. "I had to grow up very quickly, and so I always had this thing of wanting to one day escape and have my freedom, I guess," she says. Steph was always a bit audacious, never one to ride on the back of the boys' bikes as a teen. She got road-legal with a motorcycle license when she turned twenty-one. Both of her parents were riders, and she continued that tradition. In 2008 she left her career as a mortgage advisor and opened an off-road riding school in Wales. Within six months she and her business partner had attracted a contract with Honda, and within a year they were running tours in Morocco, becoming the biggest school of its kind in the UK.

When her son had grown and she felt it was time to hit the road, Steph drew a big line across a world map in her office and began researching destinations. Having dreamed of grandiose travels for more than two decades, she quickly made up her mind about the adventure. "I decided to ride to all seven continents, and a couple of tequilas convinced me I could do it," she explains. "Then I realized certain things would be more difficult. I wanted to go through China, but it was very expensive, and I would've had to have a guide, so that dictated my route a little bit." After sufficient planning, tucking away a few sentimental items in her parents' attic, and prepping her Honda CRF250L, she took off. Steph spent about six hours a day on the motorcycle, with her epic adventure covering 80,000 miles through fifty-four countries.

Her small but mighty Honda, chosen for its purpose-built dirt-loving nature, had nearly no issues

during their four-year trek through all sorts of terrain. Obviously speed is not the objective with a trip like this. "Rhonda the Honda" needed only one minor shop trip through all of their travels. It's likely that Rhonda's small stature assisted Steph in achieving her Antarctic goal, too, which many people discouraged, saying arranging bike transport would be impossible. "Antarctica was a big one for me. We managed it on a tiny sailing yacht across the notoriously rough Drake Passage." It took forty-eight hours to traverse the infamous 11,000-foot deep passage, known as one of the Earth's roughest waterways.

While her friends and family were mostly supportive of the trip, there were certain countries

and areas that caused concern. Coincidentally these were often the same places Steph found to be most rewarding. "With places like Iran, my friends and family were nervous about me going there alone, but every time I stopped, locals were trying to take me home and feed me—my biggest danger was probably getting fat." Colombia, Mexico, and Ethiopia were other favorite countries that she was initially trepidatious to visit. The adage "don't judge a book by its cover" suits such a wide variety of scenarios, doesn't it? Meanwhile India was one of the roughest on her physically, with 104°F temperatures that gave her heat exhaustion and traffic as bad as it is notorious. Overall, however, her experiences were good, and the people equally as wonderful. "I've

never really had trouble," she says. "Ninety-five percent of the people I've met have been exceptionally friendly and helpful."

So if you want to go on an incredible expedition on your own but pesky self-doubts are getting in the way, just remember that no one knows what they're doing when they first try something. Steph confesses: "Everyone had faith in me, but I was terrified. They thought I knew what I was doing, but I didn't."

Also remember that you don't need a big bike to go far, an exact route for your adventure, a return date, or even a solid plan. The right attitude will take you far. "Make people laugh," Steph advises, "then people are more willing to help you, or stop and chat with you, or make you a baguette when they're really closed. I think it's all about attitude." And, keep smiling. "Often in a crowd of people who were staring at me, it may initially appear hostile. But they're all staring because they're interested. And people kind of forget what they're doing with their face, because they're just in awe or in amazement at this sight of this crazy woman on a motorbike. If you're surrounded by people in a little village in Ethiopia, or whatever, a smile is contagious. It might sound a bit corny, but it's very, very true."

TIFFANY COATES

BRITISH ADVENTURE RIDER TIFFANY COATES and her 1992 BMW R80 GS named "Thelma" have logged over 200,000 miles during their time together. Twenty-something years, and six continents—all over the Americas, Australia, Africa, Asia, and, notably, the Mount Everest Base Camp.

Moving around is nothing new for this vagabond. "I've always been a traveler," she explains. "My dad was in the British Army and so my childhood was spent on the move." For a while, her restless feet were satisfied by backpacking. Then she found a motorized method of movement.

Most adventures begin with a dream that starts small and grows over the years until it finally hits with a bang. Tiffany's passion for traveling began with a two-up road trip with a friend. "My friend Becky and I wanted to travel to India and a spur-of-the-moment decision was made to go by bike," she says. She wasn't a motorcycle rider; in fact, she had never even owned a car. The pair took the rather rigorous five-day motorcycle training course to get their license and went on the hunt for a used bike suitable to carry both riders and their gear. Just two months after purchasing the R80GS, they loaded it up and Tiffany chopped off her locks: "A little-known fact about this trip is that I sold *all* my hair to a wig maker the night before we set off—it got us got enough money for tire levers and some other tools." With some money in their pocket and new equipment in their kit, the pair set off. They dropped their bike countless times, learning

to maneuver the tall motorcycle with a high center of gravity and loaded with luggage. "It was a baptism by fire," Tiffany says.

They intended for their excursion to last some eight months, but for Tiffany, it lasted two and a half years. Starting out in Europe, they headed through Turkey to Iran, Pakistan, and then India. When they reached their original destination, they fancied keeping on, all the way to Australia, so they hunkered down and spent some time saving up to head Down Under. When it was time to head out, Becky decided to hang back and settle down with her boyfriend. Tiffany found a new adventure buddy, Maggie, to accompany her back to Britain by way of a cross-Africa trip. Finally home, she was struck: "I realized

that I'd discovered a new passion in life: a burning desire to see more places on two wheels."

Since that original trip, she's been eating up miles. "I have also ridden from Alaska to Tierra del Fuego, to Timbuktu, to Outer Mongolia, Tokyo, across Central Asia, China, and Tibet, reaching Mount Everest Base Camp, along the Trans-Labrador Highway, around Madagascar, and many other journeys," she says. Tiffany also leads customized adventure tours, sharing her wisdom with other passionate explorers. "I would hope that people would look at me and my riding and realize that it's the desire to travel that's important rather than how much riding has been done. And that anyone can follow their dreams."

EFFIE & AVIS HOTCHKISS

This Girl Made the Double Transcontinental Trip with her Harley-Davidson and Sidecar

Miss Effie N. Hotchkiss of Brooklyn, New York, accompanied by her mother, Mrs. Avis Hotchkiss, drove across the American continent from Brooklyn to San Francisco with her three-speed twin cylinder Harley-Davidson

IMAGINE BEING HANDED A PAPER MAP AND A no-frills motorcycle and being sent on a 9,000-mile road trip in 1915. That's right—no cellphone, no GPS, no antilock brakes, poor suspension, subpar leather safety gear, and lights not much stronger than a large candle.

That's what Effie and Avis Hotchkiss were up against. Could you make it? On modern roads with signs, GPS, and frequent fuel stops, a resourceful and confident rider could do it. But most still wouldn't dare. Now imagine a time when service stations were hard to find, signage was scarce, vehicles were unreliable, and there was no AAA. Could you do it? Would you even try? These ladies did, becoming the first women to ride across America.

Effie was a motorcycle fanatic who daydreamed of motorcycle travel while working her clerical job on Wall Street. She made up her mind to go to California at twenty-six years old and brought along an unusual passenger. "I asked mother if she would come along," Effie recalls. "She said it was a good thing I did, for the next moment she would have invited herself."

Her mom Avis went along for a rather logical reason: to keep her daughter safe. Effie was quite the speed demon, and Avis wanted to keep her speed in check by adding weight to the whole outfit—a Harley-Davidson with sidecar.

JOLANDIE RUST, AKA JO RUST, IS A HISTORY-MAKING adventure rider. Born in South Africa, the thirty-something speaks three languages and is a professional off-road motorcycle instructor, tour guide, and author. The very first time she set out on the road by bike she was robbed at gunpoint, but the fierce and petite 5-foot-4 Jo didn't let it get the best of her. She went on to become the first person to ride solo around Africa, the first female marshal for the International GS Trophy, the first-ever female brand ambassador for BMW Motorrad South Africa, and the fourth internationally accredited female off-road instructor in the world and the first in Africa. She was also the fastest woman to solo bicycle from Johannesburg to Cape Town.

Her 3,500-mile bicycle trip across Africa started everything. Travel by two wheels suited her fine, but she wanted to add horsepower. In 2011 she took off for her Africa adventure on a BMW F650 GS Dakar. While she was never scared to ride solo into the unknown, Jo was faced with one of the scariest situations anyone can be put in. In northern Angola, she was held up at gunpoint by two men who took everything. Shaken but alive, she returned home to collect herself—and buy new equipment. After recuperating, she set off in April 2012 to complete her trip. A year and a half and more than 28,000 miles later, Jo became the first woman to circumnavigate Africa on a motorcycle alone.

While she faced a life-altering trauma during her first trip, it didn't change her outlook for the worse or discourage her from traveling or experiencing new cultures. "If you're a motorcycle rider, it immediately makes you a member of a very big and extensive global family!" she says. "I guess I can back this up with a story of riding in Libya, a recently war-torn country, during the Arab Spring—as a non-Arab, non-Muslim female, on my own! I was met with nothing but respect and kindness by all the motorcycle riders I met throughout the country." All of these experiences have given her a new attitude toward life and struggles: "Ever since my trip, I know that I can accomplish anything. I have become the person I always wanted to be."

DORIS WIEDEMANN'S WHEELS HAVE BEEN TURNING since 1990, when she got hooked on solo adventure riding during a five-month trip across America. Born in Munich in 1967, she holds a master's degree in economics, and her past adventures have been partially funded by her work as a tax accountant. Today she works as a journalist, PR consultant, and author of books about her travels, most notably her 2006 trip to China, where she was the first female foreigner to ride around the country without a guide.

Doris considers her start on two wheels nothing short of typical. "I had a boyfriend when I was sixteen and he rode a motorcycle and I was a passenger for two years," she explains. When she was eighteen she wanted to get her license and her own bike. Perplexed by her boyfriend's question "Why?" she carried on with her moto mission. After a weeklong trip around Bavaria on a Kawasaki Z650 B, the seed was planted.

Five years later she headed to the States with time to spare and a list of sights to see, the Grand Canyon and the fiftieth anniversary of the Sturgis Motorcycle Rally among them. Doris flew to America, bought a Honda Shadow 700, and proceeded to do 17,000 miles over the next five months. Unable to afford the transport of her new two-wheeled friend back home to Germany, their torrid affair ended with a toodle-oo. Back in Germany, she worked for three years, saving money and completing her master's degree. Finally she bought a BMW R100GS PD, which she took on an extended six-week inaugural trip through Scandinavia. With goals of further world travel on the horizon, she began tweaking her new travel companion, adding an 11-gallon fuel tank, custom aluminum side cases, and Öhlins suspension. With the upgrades in place, she shipped her Beemer buddy to Australia, which they explored for six months.

Australia led to North Africa, from which she proceeded south for seven months to Cape Town before heading east. The bike's previous owner, then living in South Korea, invited her to join him at his home. Sometimes all it takes is an open door to inspire a new destination, so Doris headed across Russia, where she caught a new ferry line from Vladivostok to South Korea. Being the first passenger with a vehicle, she set her own price for the boat ride and became the first foreign traveler to bring her own motorcycle into the country, which was illegal at the time. She was able to repeat this feat when she scooted into North Korea, a country notorious for its closed borders, for an organized ride. This made her the first non-Korean woman to travel in the country on her own motorcycle. From there she carried on to Japan, then back home to Germany by way of Russia, returning via the same road she had motored on some 25,000 miles before.

In the spring of 2005, Doris was tempted to take her beloved BMW on a trip to China when she was told she could get it across the border and ride without a guide. Warned that her motorcycle would not leave the country with her prompted some extra planning. The following year, Doris purchased a used F650GS Dakar. She crossed Poland, Ukraine, Kazakhstan, and Mongolia into China for a six-month tour. As luck would have it, the trip ended with her being able to hang on to the little GS, which she named "Redround Cheeky."

Clearly not one to shy from a challenge, her next trip was something most people wouldn't consider attempting, proven by yet another first for her collection. In January 2009, she and a partner headed out from Key West, Florida, riding to Alaska on a BMW F800GS in the dead of winter. After fighting ice-covered roads and temperatures as low as −40°F, they rolled on studded tires into Prudhoe Bay on March 2 after 13,000 miles. It's no surprise her GS is now on display in a special exhibition called "Travel Heroes" at the largest motorcycle museum in Germany, Deutsches Zweirad- und NSU-museum Neckarsulm.

So, what besides petrol fuels Doris's seemingly insatiable thirst for travel? People. "My main purpose of traveling is meeting people," she says. "My curiosity about their culture and their way of living, their language, their interests, and their humor repeatedly drag me away from my working desk." Given this, it may seem counterintuitive that her time exploring is often spent alone. "There is no familiar friend to talk to," she explains. "There is nobody to share the luggage and organizational work, the joyful and the sad moments on the road." From her perspective, however, the benefits far outweigh the moments of loneliness. Hosts often have limited space and can accommodate single travelers with much more ease, but more so, Doris has found it a better way to truly experience other cultures. "Being on my own I do integrate into their households and accommodate myself to their family life. This way I experience—absolutely subjective and without satisfying any statistical requirements—life in different countries."

These connections keep Doris Wiedemann rolling, fueling that love for heading 'round the next bend, and the next, and the next. "All over the world people are shaken with anger and disappointment, fear and sorrow. But there is also love and sympathy, joy and hospitality. Relationships between human beings are the greatest adventures of the human race. In this sense of meaning, and only in this sense, I am an adventurer."

"BELIEVE IN YOURSELF AND KICK-START THE world" is Benka Pulko's motto. Very few people can say they've set foot on every landmass on this big, wide Earth, but Benka is among the exploring elite. In fact, she was the first woman to ride her motorcycle on all seven continents. If there's anyone from whom to take motorcycle adventuring advice, it's her.

Born in a city of 20,000 in Slovenia during the Communist era, she didn't let small-town living deter her from dreaming big. She planned to become a biologist or nurse and accomplished both by young adulthood.

One morning while lying in bed, inspired by Paolo Coelho's novel *The Alchemist* and her impending thirtieth birthday, the idea hit and a decision was made in a flash. While Benka didn't own a motorcycle or even know how to ride, these seemed like minor inconveniences in the scheme of things. Five months later, in 1997, with a BMW F650 loaded up and a two-year plan on the books, she set out for what would turn into a record-breaking and life-changing road trip. (At what point does it cease being a road trip and simply become *road life*?) Over the next two thousand days, Benka moseyed along, enjoying the ride and averaging 68 miles and nine euros a day. She went through nineteen tires and ten chains, traversed seventy-five countries, and traveled just under 112,000 miles. The journey is emblazoned in *The Guinness Book of World Records* as the Longest Solo Female Motorcycle Journey. She has even been named the Slovene Woman of the Year and is known to be the first woman to ride Saudi Arabia alone.

Benka published a bestselling coffee-table book about the trip called *Po Zemlji okoli Sonca* (*Circling the Sun*). It won the top award at the Annual Slovene Book Fair, sold out of its first print run, and made its way into the hands of notables such as Barack Obama, Dolly Parton, Prince Harry, Brad Pitt, and George Clooney. Her other works include children's books, pieces in more than twenty-four newspapers and magazines, and numerous radio and podcast appearances. She also shares her knowledge of road life and solo travel with other adventure-hungry motorcyclists as a travel expert with BMW Motorrad.

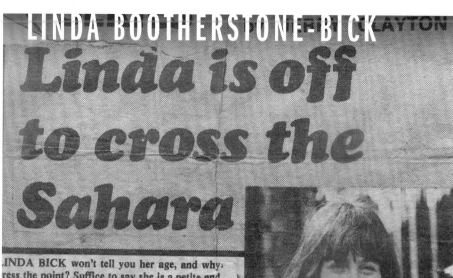

Linda is off to cross the Sahara

LINDA BICK won't tell you her age, and why press the point? Suffice to say she is a petite and very attractive brunette who has no difficulty in turning male heads wherever she goes. And, in the nicest possible way, Linda's certainly been around!

I first met Linda in 1967. We were both members of the Saltbox Motor Cycle Club and one evening she calmly announced she was off to Moscow on her 500cc Triumph Speed Twin.

The event was the BMF Moscow Rally, and despite those who said it was too long a ride for a girl, she managed comfortably and earned new respect from her male counterparts.

It came as no surprise, therefore, to find among my mail recently, a letter from Linda announcing her intention to traverse the Sahara from north to south on

IF YOU'VE EVER READ ANYTHING ABOUT LINDA Bootherstone-Bick before, it probably included the phrase "over fifty years on the road." But it's not just the length of time Linda's been riding that deserves recognition. She is a pioneer in adventure motorcycling, for men and women alike, whose travels have taken her around the globe. Her longest excursion came when she was almost sixty. Now in her mid-seventies, she's still rolling on two wheels.

Born in England, Linda got her exhilarating first rides on two wheels from a fella she met at seventeen years old. The excitement turned to trouble after a crash with her on back, but rather than turn away from motorcycles she resolved to ride her own. Her first bike was a BSA 250 she used to zip around town

and turn the heads of onlookers who were shocked, to say the least. Her next bike was a mechanically challenging Triumph Tiger Cub that broke down left and right. Owning it was sort of like motorcycle boot camp. When you get used to a junker, not only do you learn how to fix simple things, but also newer bikes become a big treat. When she moved to Australia with two friends in 1969, Linda bought a new BMW R60/5 that she piloted while the trio rode all around the continent.

In 1974 Linda set out on an incredible solo adventure around Africa on a 1957 BMW. During the fifteen-month trip she met many hardships. And not just the minor inconveniences of not having a cellphone or GPS that would debilitate many of us

these days. Add in infrequent access to clean water and electricity, cumbersome and clunky camping and survival gear, and a bout with malaria—and those don't even include challenges related to the motorcycle. Her bike's engine died and its suspension broke. Despite all that, Linda considers the trip a success, her account of which was published in her book *Into Africa with a Smile*.

In 2005, on her longest single trip, Linda rode a Suzuki DR650 from Spain to Darwin, Australia, in twenty-one months. In 2016 you would have found her wandering through Peru and Bolivia on a small bike she picked up in Santiago, Chile, and celebrating her birthday in Sucre, Bolivia's capital. After that she popped over to Argentina, back to Chile, and jetted to Glasgow with her fiddle for the Celtic Connections Festival. The following year she returned to Africa for the first time since the 1970s, heading to Uganda and Rwanda to see sights and friends. Most recently Linda and a friend took a month-long tootle from Nullarbor in South Australia to Perth to speak at the Adventure Travel Film Festival. The bikes this time? Two ex-Auspost Honda CT110s (also known as "postie" bikes), which the ladies named "Rosie-Lea" and "Mo." "Fifty years and five continents later, my bikes have been getting progressively smaller," Linda jokes. She keeps riding, she keeps smiling. Be like Linda.

RACERS & STUNTERS

THAT WHICH GIVES THE AVERAGE PERSON GREAT pause is what brings a sense of peace to the women profiled in this chapter, whether from the adrenaline or a sense of accomplishment in competition.

Fifty years ago women were denied racing licenses simply because riding wasn't a ladylike thing to do. Organizers were afraid of the bad press that could come from a woman getting injured (or worse). In 2021 we see men and women side-by-side at starting lines, competing for the same trophies. In these pages, you'll find the stories of some of the mind-blowing ladies who have soared (sometimes literally) past expectations for riders of the "fairer sex," proving, in fact, that there's no such thing.

From stunt riders slamming through fiery walls to women earning points in MotoGP, the riders in this chapter helped win respect for women riders everywhere.

VICKI GOLDEN

WATCHING THIS DAREDEVIL FLY THROUGH THE air on a dirt bike is sort of like watching a hawk dive for its prey in slow motion. Vicki Golden gets slideways with ease, pops wheelies like she gets paid for them (oh, wait, she does), and flings dirt in the faces of the fellas she races against. A San Diego native, Vicki was the first female member to race on team Metal Mulisha and the first woman to compete in Supercross. She also holds multiple records and gold medals.

In fact Vicki's made history throughout the world of motorcycle sports, from being the first woman to compete with the guys in Supercross, Arenacross, and EnduroCross, starting in 2011, to her four X-Games medals (three gold, one bronze). At this point, it's hard to say what she's most known for: her motocross career starting in 2008, being the first woman to pull off a freestyle motocross backflip (on one of the largest FMX ramps in the world), or her flaming board-bashing world record. "Bringing the heat" took on a

whole new meaning in 2019 when she donned layers of protective gear, including a Nomex fire-resistant suit, climbed onto her Indian FTR 1200, and got ready to hold her breath. In San Bernardino, California, during History Channel's "Evel Live 2" event with the Nitro Circus tour, Vicki blasted through thirteen pine boards engulfed in 30-foot flames burning at up to 2,000°F, securing herself a world record in the process.

Not everyone can be born with a throttle in their hand, but Vicki is one such lucky lady. She started racing when she was just seven years old because she saw both her brother and her dad doing it. Nine years later she was standing on the topmost spot of the podium at Loretta Lynn's Women's Amateur Championship. The same year, sixteen-year-old Vicki earned her AMA/WMX Pro license and she's been tearing up the track ever since.

"I'm out there and I'm trying to race just like every single person on the track is—because they believe they can do it," she says.

DEBBIE LAWLER

THE FIRST WOMAN MOTORCYCLIST TO BEAT an Evel Knievel record, Debbie Lawler came to be known as "The Flying Angel" and "Queen of Motorcycle Jumpers." In the mid-1970s, women were just starting to get traction in motorcycle racing, but outside of county fair–type performances (think "Wall of Death"), women were not known for stunt riding or daredevil tactics.

That is, until Debbie came along.

A former cheerleader and fashion model, Debbie was feminine, striking, and a petite 5-foot-2. These facts only made the impact of her wild nature more impressive and kept the press infatuated with her.

They called her a "tigress on a motorcycle" and "the female Evel."

Born in Grants Pass, Oregon, in 1952, Debbie was the daughter of moto racing champ Ben Lawler and took her first ride with her dad at nine years old. A few years later, after the family moved to Arizona, she was given her first motorcycle and started racing at fourteen. She began jumping in 1972, quickly earning more than she ever did in modeling. In March 1973, in Phoenix, Lawler jumped her Suzuki 76 feet over parked cars, earning a world record for "Motorcycle Distance Jumping: Female." Less than a year later in February 1974, at age twenty-

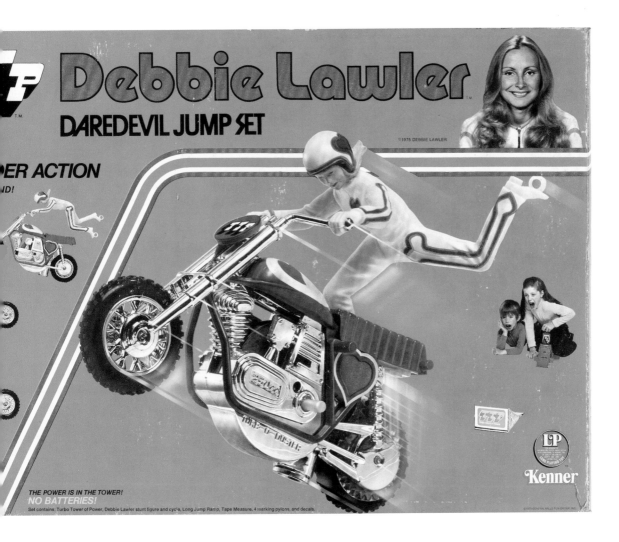

THE POWER IS IN THE TOWER!
NO BATTERIES!
Set contains: Turbo Tower of Power, Debbie Lawler stunt figure and cycle, Long Jump Ramp, Tape Measure, 4 marking pylons, and decals.

one, her 101-foot leap over sixteen Chevy trucks broke Knievel's record. The feat was broadcast live on ABC's *Wide World of Sports*, earned a spot in the *Guinness Book of World Records*, and lit the American press afire.

Knievel was less impressed, however, saying, "I can spit farther than that." One month later he reclaimed his title as biggest and baddest daredevil, jumping seventeen cars at the Portland (Oregon) Memorial Coliseum. Debbie, one of eight thousand spectators on hand, was more than a good sport, commenting, "It was a beautiful jump, just beautiful." Imagine being the woman who got Evel Knievel so

kerfuffled he had to stage a world record event just to beat you. That's Debbie Lawler.

In the following years she appeared on TV shows like *What's My Line?* and in print ads for companies such as Eagle Tires. She was also an aspiring actress and expert water-skier. Despite news outlets touting her as an old-fashioned, wholesome gal who loved kids and the elderly, her favorite food was fried chicken and she smoked two packs a day. The type of lady who lived a life she desired, not swayed by the norms of society, she also never wore a bra. Except for one. "I won't jump without my lucky bra," she once said. "It's a real dainty French thing. I'm superstitious about it."

MERCEDES GONZALEZ

MADRID-BORN MERCEDES GONZALEZ WAS A force of nature in early-'90s motocross. Her family moved to Southern California when she was a young girl, and she began riding motorcycles at age seven. This early start helped her get a leg up in the world of dirt-bike riding, leading to her being dubbed the "Fastest Woman in Motocross" in 1992. With so few women in the sport, she ended up competing against future champions like Jeremy McGrath before they went pro.

Her MX career came before the Women's Motocross Championship was formed, but she dominated in various men's divisions, specializing women's classes and backed by Kawasaki for much of her time tearing up the dirt.

Mercedes is one of the most decorated female racers to this day, with five Loretta Lynn championships and nine national championships. When she felt that her time was done, she turned to the four-wheel world for thrills. "I guess after racing and winning for eight years, I felt that I either needed to compete against guys on the pro level or just move on," Gonzalez said. In 1993 she began racing in the Mickey Thompson off-road series Superlight class

with teammate Jimmie Johnson (he of NASCAR renown). At Denver's Mile High Stadium she became the first woman to win a series event.

Next she dabbled in downhill mountain bike racing and held her own against much younger competitors, taking home the silver at the 1995 UCI Mountain Bike World Championship downhill competition in Germany and the bronze in both the European championship in Italy the following year and the Spanish championship in 1998. She retired from racing at thirty-six and is now the mother of two teenage boys. She organizes and runs programs and staff schedules at the Honda Rider Education Center in California, where they provide entry-level training with dirt bikes, ATVs, and side-by-sides to families and private groups.

LIKE MANY PROFESSIONAL MOTORCYCLE RACERS, Avalon Biddle got her start at a super young age. Born in Auckland, New Zealand, in 1992, she started riding a Yamaha PW50 at age six, racing minimotocross with her older brother. At thirteen she began road racing at the local go-kart track, quickly winning a "Most Promising Newcomer Award." Her track skills convinced her parents to keep her moving forward in racing, so they bought a Suzuki RG150 that she rode

in the highly competitive nationwide 150 Street Stock class. "After numerous wins and breaking a lap record, we decided that traveling to Australia to race would provide me with some stronger competition to gain more experience and realize my potential," she recalls. "I finished fifth in the 2007 Australian Motorcycle Road Race Development Association (MRRDA) series."

Avalon has continued to rack up the wins since her beginnings as a wee lass, including second overall

in the Italian Women's Championship on a Honda CBR600rr, champion in the 2015 New Zealand Superlite, champion in the 2015 and 2016 FIM European Women's Cup, and first woman to win a 600cc National Championship race in NZSBK (New Zealand Superbike) in 2018. The following year she won three more times in the same Supersport class and became the New Zealand Supersport 600cc champion at twenty-six . . . another first for a woman!

These days she's still racing Supersport, working in marketing, cohosting a TV show called *Skyspeed*, and writing for a motorcycle magazine. Avalon is also studying for her business degree and keeping herself sharp for the track. It's obvious we've got a lot to look out for from Avalon in the future.

TARAH GIEGER, A NATIVE PUERTO RICAN WHO'S spent most of her life in Florida, was the first woman to win a gold medal in a motorcycle event at the X Games and the first woman to backflip a motorcycle. When her parents relocated from Aguadilla to America, they brought their surf shop with them. Basically born on a board and riding the waves, Tarah developed a love for extreme sports that was nurtured from a young age. Her career, beginning in 2003, is a long list of wins—and broken bones.

Tarah started riding at ten years old when her dad got her a bike. "It was just something I wanted to mess around on, and he was all about it," she recalls. "Originally I wanted a go-kart because kids in my neighborhood had them, but those are pretty dangerous." This seems like something only Tarah would say!

Not one to back down from a challenge, Tarah has never been hindered by fear. "That's just how I am," she says. "Stuff doesn't scare me. When we went out on dirt bikes, I'd be the one to hit the jumps. Everyone else would be scared, and I'd go for it."

After growing up playing baseball and surfing like "one of the boys," she found the competitive atmosphere Stateside to be a new experience. She says that the boys would try harder to pass her when she first started racing—seeing hair come out of the back of the helmet would give them a second wind. "But that's changed over the years. Now it's not really a big deal when a girl is better."

This unstoppable woman's start in racing wasn't the smoothest. She's been racking up wins since 2003, but not without some pain along the way. She took the Loretta Lynn AMA Amateur National Motocross Championship titles in 2004, 2006, and 2007. What about 2005? Well, it started off with shattering her pelvis when she fell in a race and another rider landed on her. After two months in a wheelchair, she got

right back on that horse, starting in the outdoor series. She quickly was in the running to take home the championship, but while in the lead of race four, she high-sided and got thrown over her bars. "I woke up in an ambulance with a broken neck and was out another eight months," she says. "So that was a tough year." The downtime healing really tested her dedication. She thought about quitting, but when the doctors gave her the all-clear, she "was ready to get back out there and show everybody who said I wouldn't that they didn't know who I was."

One of Tarah's most famous (read: mainstream) appearances was in *ESPN the Magazine*'s 2013 Body Issue, where she was featured in "Bodies We Want." The whole moto world was aflutter when the pictures dropped of her tearing up the track in the buff. Tarah's happy to show off what she's worked so hard for. She's in the gym four days a week and her training includes everything from the obvious, like riding motocross, to favorite pastimes like surfing and more unconventional standup Jet Skis.

Whatever she's doing is working. Tarah's been on the podium at every major event in which she's participated, soared to great heights with Nitro Circus, and succeeded in her goal of dominating women's motocross. "My goal is to win everything I enter,"

she comments. In 2007 she became the first woman to ever compete in the Motocross des Nations, an annual race often referred to as the "Olympics of Motocross." The following year, she took gold at the very first women's Moto X event at the X Games. More injuries were upon her in 2010 when she broke her wrist, but in true Tarah spirit she competed in a bunch of world championship races anyway. Perhaps it was this dedication, or more likely a culmination, of all she'd done that paid off when she joined the Troy Lee Design/Lucas Oil/Honda racing team in 2010, a precursor to double silver medals at the X Games Super X. The winning streak continues with a long list of shiny medals and awards, including the 2019 AMA National Grand Prix champion.

So what's the secret? "Doubting yourself is your worst enemy," she advises. "Every time you line up to race, you have to push that back."

BRITTNEY OLSEN

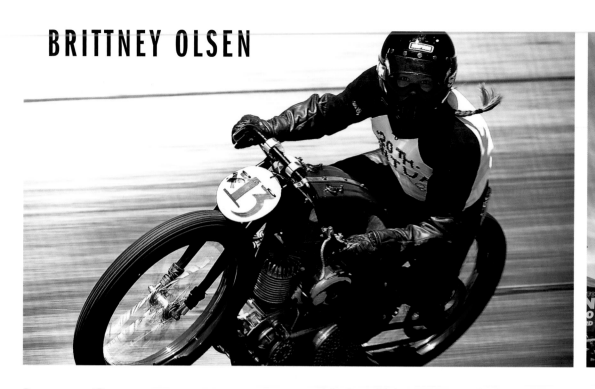

BRITTNEY OLSEN IS NOT YOUR TYPICAL motorcycle racer. She doesn't go for the newest, fastest thing. She likes them rough, rusty, and old. Growing up in South Dakota in the '90s, she was a tear on go-karts and gave her dad the idea to get her going on something bigger. With her dad's help she saved up for a two-stroke quad and pretty quickly got to putting the smackdown on boys and men alike. These days her goals are to keep historic racing alive and to preserve America's motorcycle history. Happily the two go hand in hand—or, rather, hand in throttle.

Everything began when Brittney met three-time NHRA World Champion drag racer Shirley Muldowney at just three years old. A racer was born. She started out at eleven racing ATVs before moving on to drag racing her dad's 1969 Camaro at fourteen and then the antique motorcycle racing she does now. She learned to wrench with her dad as she went, and one of her first notable builds was a little green motorized Schwinn Pea Picker they built in their living room when she was seventeen. It was originally a Christmas present for her brother, but for years to come they used it as a pit bike at the dragstrip, getting lots of compliments. In 2009 they took it to the Sturgis Motorcycle Rally, where she met Pat Patterson (Led Sled Customs) and Chris Callen (*Cycle Source* magazine), who embraced her (literally) for building such a rad machine. They encouraged her craftsmanship and racing, saying the motorcycling world needed more women. It started a wonderful friendship. In the coming years, Brittney spent time with Pat and Chris, refining her interests in racing. "I remember seeing a 1917 Excelsior board-track racer and falling in love with the simple design," she recalls. "I looked up more board-trackers and found out that they were just like my motorized bicycle! I also found out that they were going a hundred miles an hour in the teens, which was mind-blowing." Brittney had discovered her deep love for antique motorcycles and building bikes.

Her eye for style isn't limited to rolling art. This speed demon and lover of rumbly bikes is a sight on

and off the track. If you spot her at events, she'll likely be wearing period-correct clothing, complete with pantaloons (usually made of straight wool) and cap. This penchant for style, combined with her flair for the fast and old, has made her an iconic woman in the modern motorcycling era.

In 2017, Brittney received *Cycle Source*'s Woman of the Year award and was an AIMExpo National Ambassador the same year. Her racing victories include AMA Sturgis Half-Mile champion in 2014, 2015, and 2016; 2015 AMA Pro Black Hills Half-Mile champion; and the first champion of the inaugural Sons of Speed Vintage Races at Daytona Bike Week 2017. In 2019 she was invited to the Goodwood Festival of Speed in England to display her 1923 champion Harley-Davidson J model and her 1928 Indian board-tracker in its big debut. "To be invited over as an American champion truly allowed me to see that I had achieved my dreams of being recognized as a racer," she says. "Not only just a standard hobby racer but a top American antique motorcycle racer." If you missed

her on the track you may have seen her on the Travel Channel, in the *Wall Street Journal*, or immortalized in amazing fine art paintings by David Uhl.

Brittney works with her fellow racers and community to help keep vintage motorcycle racing alive—for the love of it, for her local town of Sturgis, for the history. She founded the Spirit of Sturgis Racing Festival, a series of vintage racing events set up to run alongside the town's yearly rally we all know so well. It takes place at the historical Sturgis Half-Mile, which Brittney herself rallied to preserve. "My favorite thing about racing old bikes is the camaraderie and people involved. All of us together are working our hardest to preserve American motorcycle racing history."

Good times shared on and off the track between racers, bonds built in banging metal, and laughs around the fire are timeless. They're important parts of not just motorcycle history, but American history.

SHELINA MOREDA IS A FARM GIRL FROM northern California who's been on two wheels since she was twelve. Chores on the dairy farm in Petaluma were done on motorcycle whenever possible. "My dad never knew what he was starting when he made us do chores on the motorcycles, like bringing the cows in from the fields," she muses. Since then she's been riding and racing all over the world, running girls' off-road moto camps, leading an emergency livestock fire evacuation team, and becoming an official Covergirl.

Her pro-level racing career has taken her across America and Europe, to Japan, Qatar, and China. Shelina has a lot of firsts under her belt. She was part of the first female team to complete a Suzuka endurance race, the first woman to race a motorcycle at Indianapolis Motor Speedway, the first woman to race at the Zhuhai International Circuit in China, the first woman to race the Harley XR1200 series, and finished first in the 2016 Women's Qatar Supersport Championship.

She'z Racing, Shelina's company, runs She'z Moto Camps in the sprawling dairy fields of her hometown. It's an all-female, all-ages motorcycle school that doesn't just teach riding skills but also encourages building confidence and learning at your own pace. While the school focuses on the gals, they're sure to host family events where everyone can learn together. Two days with hands-on training from Shelina runs riders of all ages through drills and classes, shaping the future of motorcycling in a very direct way.

Shelina's got a sparkling personality, her eyes light up when she smiles (which is often), and she's incredibly kind. Perhaps that's what helped her become a Covergirl. And really, how cool is that—a petrol-fueled, speed-loving, two-wheeler representing one of the world's top makeup brands? That's one thing ladies like Shelina really kick into gear: a mainstream realization that you can be both feminine *and* fast.

ASHLEY FIOLEK'S RACING CAREER WAS AS impressive as it was short. Born deaf in Michigan in 1990, she and her family relocated to St. Augustine so that she could attend the Florida School for the Deaf and Blind, where she participated in activities from ballet to basketball. Family trips back to her grandfather's cabin introduced her to motorcycles. Like so many of the most impressive motorcyclists, she was given a little dirt bike—a Yamaha PW50— when she was just three. She started racing at seven,

and by the time she was eighteen she went pro—hard and fast. Ashley flew in without brakes, whooped a bunch of boys, and wheelied out just as fast in 2012.

Called the most influential female motocross rider of all time, Ashley spent a brief time racing but has had a long-lasting influence: During her time as a pro, she became the first woman signed to the American Honda Factory racing team; was the first female racer on the cover of *TransWorld Motocross* magazine; was nominated for an ESPN ESPY award;

was featured in a Red Bull commercial; made it into the pages of *Vogue, Rolling Stone*, and *Sports Illustrated*; and presented a TEDx Talk. She was an X Games double gold medalist, and her first win in Women's Super X made her the first deaf medalist at the games. She was also the first deaf person to appear on *Conan* in 2012, and she made an appearance in the award-winning drama *Switched at Birth*. Perhaps most notably, Ashley took home four Women's Motocross (WMX) Pro National championships.

At twenty-one, Ashley decided to leave the world of motocross behind. She still rides, and sometimes races, working in recent years with companies like Fox Racing and Husqvarna as a brand ambassador. But mainly she focuses on spreading her passion for motorcycles by training riders through the Ashley Fiolek MX School.

KERRY KLEID & DEBBI SELDEN

SPECIFICATIONS		
	250cc	**360cc**
Model	980	969/01
Bore	70mm	80mm
Stroke	64mm	72mm
Compression Ratio	10.5:1	10.5:1
Horsepower	29 @ 6,800 rpm	36 @ 6,400 rpm
Dry Weight	227 lbs.	234 lbs.
POE List Price	$1075	$1225

IN 1970, NEW YORK NATIVE KERRY KLEID applied for and was granted an AMA Pro Motocross license. While commonplace today, it was unheard of at the time. Across the oceans, a handful of other race associations allowed women to compete in the early '70s, but not the American Motorcycle Association. Kerry's ambiguous first name allowed the paperwork to slide through the bureaucratic cracks. But when she showed up for an AMA Pro Motocross race in July 1971 in Unadilla, New York, she wasn't allowed to enter. Realizing she was in fact a woman, the AMA yanked her license. A lawsuit was filed in Manhattan Federal Court soon after.

A few years earlier, in 1968, teenage motocross racer Debbi Selden of Tacoma, Washington, had sent a petition to the AMA requesting she be given a pro license when she turned eighteen. In a *Cycle News West* article she said, "[They] don't even want to discuss it. . . . I want to race professionally though and I don't really understand why the AMA doesn't want women to compete with the men on an equal basis. Women compete in many sports. . . . The fact that I'm a girl doesn't seem to me to be a good reason for barring me from a professional license." In 1969 Selden turned eighteen, applied for an

AMA license, and was denied. Like Kleid, she filed a lawsuit.

Both women put up a fight in and out of court—nearly simultaneously and on opposite sides of the country. Selden won her case in April 1969, but the AMA quickly appealed. Around the same time, Kleid received a recommendation from Congressman Don Pink and the AMA conceded. Shortly after, the AMA also folded their case against Selden, paid her court fees, and awarded her a license.

A few short months later, in October, the AMA was boasting about Kerry's license and placing her on the cover of their *American Motorcyclist* magazine and featuring her in the article "Women in the Pits and on the Track." In November the AMA Competition Congress voted to allow "qualified women to compete in all forms of AMA racing."

In January the following year, Debbi Selden competed against the third woman to get her AMA Pro Racing license, going head-to-head with Sammy Dunn at an event in Philadelphia. Debbi won, becoming the first woman racer to reach the semis. That year she also became the first woman to race pro flat track.

MELISSA PARIS

MELISSA PARIS IS A SOUTHERN CALIFORNIA—based Superbike racer, team owner, dirt rider, entrepreneur, and mother. She is as fierce as she is fast—it's no wonder ESPN titled an article about her "The Tom Petty song that reminds motorcycle racer Melissa Paris she 'won't back down.'"

In the world of motorcycle racing, most riders smashing records and smacking down opponents got their start at a very young age. Paris, however, didn't get on a bike until she was twenty. The delay didn't diminish her talent. Married to MotoGP and MotoAmerica champion racer Josh Hayes, she was deliberate in not using his fame to her benefit when she began racing in 2005. Now in her mid-thirties, she's had many successes on track, starting in 2009 when she became the first woman to qualify for a Supersport World race, the FIM World Superbike Championship.

In the years following, Melissa participated in the British Superbike series and became the first and only woman to ever test a MotoGP M1 prototype race bike. She finished top ten at the Daytona 200 in 2013, and the next year finished fifth overall in the Spanish FIM CEV Superstock Championship. In 2014 she joined team SynergyForce in Japan for the Suzuka 4 Hours Endurance race with Shelina Moreda, Nita Korhonen, and Midori Moriwaki. The quartet became the first all-female team to finish, and while they qualified in the low sixties, they finished 28th. (To top it off, Shelina and Melissa only had a day to get familiar with the Honda CBR600RR.) In 2015 Melissa became the WERA West

Superbike champion, gained traction in MotoAmerica events, and took first place in 24 Hours of Barcelona. She is no wimp when it comes to endurance riding, and her teams in the 2016 Bol d'Or 24-hour and the 2017 Le Mans 24-hour were the first all-female teams to qualify and complete the events.

Big into flat track and motocross, Melissa founded the MP13 racing team in 2017 to help grow the sport by mentoring young riders—especially girls. The idea is to promote young talent and give kids the tools they need to get into racing (and be competitive). One of the team riders, Jamie Astudillo, has been competitive in the MotoAmerica Junior Cup, KTM RC390 Cup, and WMX World Championship.

But young 'uns on the MP13 race team aren't the only fast kids under Melissa's influence. Now a mom, she was racing while four months pregnant (something she kept to herself while on track but later shared on social pages, getting mixed reactions). While not everyone approved of her informed decision to keep racing while her bun was baking, Melissa continued riding until her leather suit wouldn't fit. She doesn't feel like a thrill seeker so much as an athlete, and racing is not just her job but also her passion. "I feel safer racing on a racetrack at triple-digit speeds than I probably do driving my car down the interstate in LA," she says.

"THE MORE YOU KNOW, THE BETTER IT GETS" is a tagline of Motoress, a website for women motorcyclists founded by Vicki Gray in 1998. Originally called Racegirl Motorsport and based in Europe, it was the first-ever website for women riders. Since then, Vicki has clocked over 1,000,000 miles, founded the very successful International Female Ride Day event, and continued working as a motorcycle instructor. She is passionate about promoting safe and fun motorcycling through her website, as well as providing hands-on training. She's taught tips and tricks of everything from road racing with former MotoGP racer Katja Poensgen to riding techniques for police in the Caribbean. Some of her other projects include cohosting the 2004 Discovery Channel pilot *Biker Girls: Born to Be Wild* and putting together the very first all-women's track sessions at the Assen TT circuit in the Netherlands.

KATJA POENSGEN

KATJA POENSGEN WAS THE FIRST WOMAN TO qualify for a 250cc Grand Prix motorcycle race and the third woman to race in the MotoGP series.

Born in Mindelheim, Germany, in 1976, Katja began her racing career when she got on a bike at four years old. Her dad, a German importer for Suzuki and a former motocross and endurance rider, made sure Katja got an early start. She officially started racing in 1993 in the ADAC Junior Cup, followed quickly in 1995 by becoming the first woman to win the Junior Cup in Germany (on a Suzuki RGV250) and then the European Supermono Cup (on a Suzuki DR650).

Since competing in the Grand Prix in the early 2000s, Katya has worked as a sports commentator, races rallycross and electric motorcycles, and continues to ride. In 2011 she was named an "FIM Legend" for her renowned groundwork for women motorcyclists.

DEBBIE EVANS

DEBBIE EVANS IS AN AMA HALL OF FAME—inducted motocross and trials rider. Born in 1958, she started on two wheels at the wee age of six and became a trailblazer in off-road motorcycling. In the late 1970s, teenage Debbie was the best female motorcycle trials rider in America. At just nineteen she got her first job as a stunt rider for the movie *Deathsport*, where she jumped a Yamaha DT400 30 feet over a ravine. Debbie was the first woman to obtain expert classification in trials, and was known for a trick where she'd balance, kickstand up, in a headstand on the seat.

Now that Debbie is one of Hollywood's most popular stuntwomen, you've probably seen her in movies, even though you may not have known it. If you saw *The Matrix: Reloaded, Taxi,* or *The Fast and the Furious*, you've seen Debbie in action. During the filming of *The Matrix: Reloaded*, she wore a tight vinyl suit with only a layer of spandex underneath in case of a crash. Debbie was hit head-on by a car during the filming and taken to the hospital with only minor injuries despite the 50-mph collision sans helmet or protective gear. All the coolest jobs come with the highest risks, it seems, and Debbie's fearlessness has allowed her to accomplish great things.

IF YOU'VE HEARD OF NITRO CIRCUS, YOU MAY have already heard of Jolene Van Vugt. And if you haven't, get ready to be amazed. Her fame really all started with her history-making backflip on a full-size dirt bike while coached by friend and FMX legend Travis Pastrana.

Pastrana had been looking for a female stunt rider to add to the Nitro Circus and Jolene was perfect. She was raised watching her dad and older brother riding motocross, and when she was eleven she convinced her parents to buy her a bike of her own. By fourteen she seemed to have lost some interest in riding and her parents told

her to practice or the motorcycle was gone. Her determination didn't waver again, which, along with her skill, were what Pastrana found so encouraging about Jolene. By the time they met in 2005, she had already become a two-time CMRC Motocross Ladies Ontario Provincial champion.

Growing up in Canada and fantasizing about becoming a Hollywood stuntwoman, Jolene was on the way to her dreams coming true. As her career with Nitro Circus grew she became known as Nitro Girl. She's jumped out of planes, backflipped her dirt bike into the Grand Canyon, set a motorized *toilet* land-speed record (46.6 mph) that earned her a

Guinness World Record, and earned another one for completing the longest tandem motorcycle backflip (16 feet 5 inches) with Pastrana. She also earned yet another Guinness World Record for the longest motorcycle backflip by a woman.

Later all these skills coalesced perfectly for a crazy cool stunt role: Catwoman in *The Dark Knight Rises* (2012). The motorcycle was hyperfuturistic and not at all easy to ride. Stunt coordinator Tom Struthers found it difficult for riders to master the bike. "A lot of very talented motorcycle guys couldn't ride the Batpod," he says. Jolene had just three days to figure it out, and she did it with ease. For four

months she donned a Lycra catsuit complete with some extra safety padding and a helmet with a wig.

Outside of stunt riding and wild shenanigans, Jolene also became the 2007 CMRC Women's Canadian National champion, competed in the 2013 X Games, and continues to race in various events like the AMA's SuperHooligan series.

"I can say with enough fire, passion, and commitment, we can all live the lives we were born to live," she says.

ERIN SILLS

POWERHOUSE—THAT'S THE WORD THAT COMES TO to mind when describing Erin Sills. A corporate business executive and forty-five-time land-speed record holder, Erin makes one wonder: does she ever stop moving? Does she do everything at over two hundred miles per hour? Erin has worked at Procter & Gamble, been on the leadership team of two internet startups, and was formerly a director at Facebook for Business. She sits on the boards of the AMA Heritage Foundation and is the co-chairwoman of WomenRidersNow.com, the number one resource for women and motorcycling. She's also a lead instructor at one of the world's top off-road motorcycle training schools, RawHyde Adventures. But wait, there's more. Erin is involved with Fédération Internationale de Motocyclisme, aka the International Motorcycling Federation

(FIM), a global governing and sanctioning body of motorcycle racing. So, ladies, she's got your backs.

In addition to her activity in the motorcycle industry, Erin is Guinness Book of World Records' fastest female on a conventional motorcycle and rides the world's fastest BMW motorcycle, hitting a top speed of 242 miles per hour (so far). On the books, however, she and the nitrous-powered BMW S1000RR (on which her late husband previously set the record) hold a world record for 237.275 miles per hour in the partial streamliner class. In all she has set over forty-five land-speed records, including a second Guinness World Record for the fastest tandem ride. She and her late husband Andy once piloted the BMW at Bonneville, taking turns as pillion so it wasn't just "the girl on the back"— hitting 181.426 miles per hour two-up!

"The First Lady of Fast" Marcia Holley was once the fastest woman in the world on two wheels. Her 229.361-mph record, set on a single-engine streamliner motorcycle, held for over thirty years. At an SCTA (Southern California Timing Association) event at the Bonneville Salt Flats in September 1978, land-speed legend Don Vesco disconnected one of two KZ1000 engines and put stunt rider Holley aboard. She rode the "Lightning Bolt" Vesco Kawasaki streamliner more than 4 miles across the Utah salt flats, breaking a land-speed record and becoming the first woman to officially break into the 200-mph club.

As a Hollywood stunt rider, she's appeared in more than fifty films, including *Total Recall, Ferris Bueller's Day Off, Reservoir Dogs,* and *Titanic,* to name a few. These days you can still find her at speed trials across America, supporting up-and-coming record-breaking women.

SHAYNA TEXTER

WHILE SOME WOMEN RACERS BROKE BARRIERS becoming competitive in ladies' classes, Shayna Texter lays it down right alongside the boys. That's not to downplay any of the incredible accomplishments of our motorcycle foremothers, it's just to note how far we've come. Just fifty years ago, women were fighting for their own AMA pro-racing licenses—now they're launching off the starting line in coed competitions left and right. The slight size of many women racers has them looking like underdogs, making wins all the more satisfying.

Challenging high-speed racing on the dirt oval track is in Shayna's blood. Born in Willow Street, Pennsylvania, a small town about an hour and a half west of Philadelphia, she got her start on two wheels at the tender age of three, no doubt influenced by her grandpa and father, both flat track racers themselves. With her dad owning a Harley-Davidson dealership, Shayna was no stranger to things that are fast, loud, and heavy. This comes in handy in a sport where she regularly power slides through long corners at ninety

miles per hour. With traction that is sometimes neither here nor there, banging bars and crashes are regular features of flat track. And much like with demolition derbies or monster truck rallies, the carnage—or at least the high likelihood of it—can be the most exciting part. Shayna knows she chose one of the most ostentatious and unforgiving competitions. "Makes you think about it twice," she admits. "But we were born to be motorcycle racers. We know what can happen and the risks, but I kinda think that's why you go out and enjoy every ride."

Her indomitable spirit, on top of both natural-born and trained talent, no doubt gives her an edge, but if Shayna were ruled by fear, she would never have ripped a throttle to begin with. When her brother Cory began racing in 2003, twelve-year-old Shayna joined in. She didn't even have a proper bike, but with a little improvisation (some tires from a streetbike mounted on her trail bike), off she rode.

In 2009 Shayna competed in the AMA Pro Singles division, finishing third in both the Springfield (Illinois)

Mile and the Kingsport (Tennessee) Half-Mile, placing her ninth overall. After her initial taste of victory in a big race, her dad's health went downhill. On the day of his passing in 2010, Shayna looked at her brother and said, "Let's go . . . we're going racing." She was struggling, at rock bottom, but she continued to push.

Then in 2011 something big happened: she dominated. Shayna became the first woman to win a flat track main event in the AMA National Pro Singles Championship. Since then, she's done so fifteen more times, becoming the "winningest American Flat track Singles rider ever." Please note there is no gender qualifier in this title. Each year since her big win in 2011, she's been seen on the podium more and more. Three wins in 2012, three more the following year, all the way up to five in 2017. In 2018 she formed her own team, backed by Husqvarna in their first foray into flat track. They tore the Husky out of the crate just days before the infamous Daytona TT, wrenching away to get the machine ready for race day. Shayna only had an hour to practice with her new bike before the start,

and it definitely wasn't enough. Even though she didn't qualify for the main event, she kept on keeping on. She went on to get three wins later in the season, which gave her the opportunity to be a part of the Red Bull KTM team in 2019.

At 5 feet and 95 pounds, Shayna is a big force in a small package, undeniably adding to spectator interest. Publications like *ESPN, Forbes,* the *Wall Street Journal,* and the *New York Times* have covered Shayna, marveling at her accomplishments as a female athlete. And while that's understandable (heck, this whole book is doing it in a way), she doesn't want to be known as "fast for a girl," just fast. Perhaps this sort of attitude, combined with her down-to-earth demeanor, is what makes her such a spectacle in the sport. Not to mention an all-around amazing ambassador for a future generation of riders.

THE WALL OF DEATH IS AN INFAMOUS AND awe-inspiring part of historic and modern-day motorcycling. Back before we had entertainment flying at us from every direction—before phones, before TV, before (*gasp*) the internet—people flocked to fairs and carnivals for excitement. Oftentimes great feats of bravery were performed by a few daring souls, usually saddled up near the sideshow. Imagine hearing the sputtering grunts and subsequent roar of rudimentary motorcycles gaining speed across rickety wood boards that creaked and shifted under the force. If you've been lucky enough to see one of these performances in person, you know firsthand that it remains every bit as impressive even in this day and age.

Kerri Cameron is one of the few women on Earth to ride the Wall of Death. It was never a customary practice for ladies, even in the Wall's heyday. Instead, we were usually relegated to riding the roller bikes out front of the entrance to attract onlookers, showing off feats of balance and coordination while 500-pound motorcycles moved in place. Certainly some women transitioned from biker billboards to stunt riders, but considering the current number of women in motorcycling (about 14 percent of all riders), this was a rarity. Kerri is keeping the tradition alive and laying it down for the gals as the first female rider in the Ken Fox Troupe history.

PLATINUM BLONDE, ANIMAL PRINT, AND NEON lights. If Ewa Pieniakowska, aka Ewa Stunts, has a brand, that's the imagery it conjures. Ewa's a Polish freestyle stunt rider who started stunt training in 2010. At just under 5-foot-5 and weighing in at 105 pounds, she's got a sort of one-two-punch approach to motorcycling. That is, she muscles bikes around like a ballerina. As in 400-pound sportbikes with over 130 horsepower. "Every show, trick, photoshoot, video, interview, and so on requires an enormous amount of energy, preparation, discipline," she told K&N in an interview. "You're always learning—and you have to learn fast."

While stunt riders throw motorcycles around like a pizza maker does dough, their feats aren't generally measured in competitive settings. Ewa doesn't have a deluge of speed records under her belt, nor championships to boast. Instead let's focus on the goodwill she's brought to the sport of motorcycling via being a positive ambassador and representative for women—and motorcyclists—everywhere. Growing up in a small town in Poland, she always had her eye on women on motorcycles, and she chased after her dreams until she was a master of her craft.

Ewa is one of the only professional Polish freestyle streetbike athletes. With her bright smile and pink gear, it's not surprising she draws a lot of attention. She's the only female to have performed in a stunt show at NitrOlympX at the Hockenheim race circuit (in front of some fifty thousand spectators), was a special guest at the Italian EICMA industry event, and represented ICON Motorsports at INTERMOT in Germany. Ewa says she's signed more than fifty thousand autographs and high-fived more than forty thousand fans.

123

CREATORS

"THIS WORLD IS BUT A CANVAS TO OUR IMAGINATION."
–HENRY DAVID THOREAU

ARTISTS ARE AN INTEGRAL PART OF ANY community, exploring ideas and controversies, and pushing boundaries to open minds. They take in the world and digest all its intricacies, relating it back through all types of media—some choose a pencil, paint, or metal, others the camera. The women in this chapter are visual catalysts, often working in the background of the motorcycle industry. Their art infiltrates and informs magazines, custom motorcycle shows, marketing campaigns, and trends in the world of motorcycles. Their efforts have helped spur the quickly growing number of women motorcyclists. Their work—fueled by their passion for adventure, friendship, nature, and love of two wheels—inspires viewers to chase these passions themselves.

Art and motorcycles have a lot in common. Both stir up things in us that are difficult to put into words. They help us transcend the mundane, soak up moments that most don't even realize they're missing, gain new perspectives, and appreciate the world.

126

A TRULY SELFLESS PERSON IS A RARITY. COMBINE that with boss welding and fabrication skills, a solid sense of self, an amazing eye for design, an in-depth understanding of mechanics, and endless energy to help friends and you get Sofi Tsingos.

Years ago, Sofi's first charity motorcycle build was featured on the MotoLady website, and it was the beginning of an amazing friendship. It's hard not to be in awe of Sofi. Even without meeting her, you get the vibe that she's warm, friendly, hilarious, giving. And all of those things are true. She continually promotes everyone else's accomplishments over her own. She takes no shit yet somehow also has endless patience. And she's a badass rider.

From building engines to banging out body dents in old cars, Sofi has been up to her elbows in all things automotive since she was a wee lass. Her father, George, an airplane mechanic and salesman by trade, never treated her "like a girl." When Mother's Day rolls around, Sofi says thanks to her dad. He did it all as a single parent, and the two were basically inseparable. Many nights of her childhood were spent in the garage with a wrench in her hand, whether or not she knew what to do with it. Sofi's dad taught her the basic workings of pretty much anything that moved under mechanical power. When Sofi was eight she had the opportunity to hop on a 1980s Honda XR80. Street riding and track days became a fixture of Sofi's life. When she was sixteen she would head to the track with her dad, laying it down with the guys, her long braid blowing in the wind.

In 2007 Sofi moved from her hometown outside Dallas, Texas, to Reno, Nevada, then to northern California in 2008 with her beau at the time. When she decided to become a certified European motorcycle technician in 2009, she packed up her stuff and headed to Daytona, Florida, picking up her dad George on the way. He had been battling cancer for two years and

she had just found out. In Florida they started their first build together, a Triton café racer.

After completing her education, she and her dad moved to New Hampshire, where she started work for a Ducati dealership. Perhaps it was the boredom of cold winters, but this is when Sofi started her first build. Her blue 1977 Honda 550 turned 605cc café racer was outfitted with a monoshock and Benelli tank, the beginning of an iconic style—and she didn't even know it. But the weather wore on Sofi and her dad, so they decided to return home in 2011. Again she got work at a Ducati dealership, but this time finding herself chained to a desk rather than getting her hands greasy. All the while, George's health was going downhill.

Troubled times hit hard in 2012 when George was given four months to live. Sofi decided her dad wasn't going to die of cancer, and she had an idea to keep his mind off the fight ahead of him. Shortly after, the pair started GT-Moto, a sort of happenstance play on the initials of George Tsingos and Gran Turismo, a nonprofit organization to build and raffle bikes off for charity. Their first project was a 1972 Honda CB450 that got a frame-up rebuild, also outfitted with a monoshock and Benelli tank.

After growing increasingly tired of her job, and with her time tied up with her new motorcycle charity projects and her dad's treatments, Sofi left dealership work to pursue her dreams of designing, fabricating, and building motorcycles. GT-Moto became an LLC in 2013

and their charity projects have continued. On top of hundreds of hours in free labor and tens of thousands in cash spent on parts and transportation, Sofi has raised over $70,000 for various charities, the primary being St. Jude Children's Hospital. The GT-MotoLady Project of 2017, a joint effort between GT-Moto and MotoLady, raised $25,000 by raffling off an MV Agusta Brutale 800 online. That bike and other GT-Moto builds have been featured in the Los Angeles–based Women's Motorcycle Show, won awards at the International Motorcycle Show (IMS) J&P Cycles custom show circuit, and been featured in countless publications internationally. And you can find a GT-Moto Yamaha XS650 custom built for and on display at the Haas Moto Museum & Sculpture Gallery in Dallas.

These days you can find Sofi perfecting her craft at a hot rod shop, working on car restoration and customization with metal shaping, and finding new projects to work on with her dad. Don't worry, she's still heavily involved in the motorcycle scene, especially when it comes to charitable work. After all, a rising tide lifts all boats. Bike builds have become more of a hobby, allowing her to focus her attention on the places that matter most—working alongside Krystal Hess, founder of Motorcycle Missions, a nonprofit that focuses on helping veterans with PTSD through motorcycle therapy.

If you're into big off-road trucks and capable crawlers à la the King of the Hammers race, you may have already heard of Theresa Contreras. She's a force in the four-wheel world, and that resonates in her passion and involvement in the motorcycle industry. She's incredibly talented with pinstriping brushes, an airbrush, a wrench, behind the wheel of pretty much any vehicle, and on any bike. That's Theresa.

Spend some time in this gal's presence and you will find yourself laughing loudly and learning much. Theresa started the Real Deal with Jessi Combs, an organization that celebrates women in the trades by giving folks the opportunity to try them hands-on at motorcycle and automotive events. Jessi was in charge of welding and fabrication; Theresa would help ladies figure out the fundamentals of the old-school art of pinstriping. As the organization grew, they invited other women who were masters of their craft to join and teach new skills like blacksmithing and leathercraft.

The Real Deal wasn't a thrown-together idea created on a whim either. This fact was obvious when looking at their booth. Designed and built by Theresa and Jessi, it features flourished, laser-cut steel corner brackets, wooden beams, and sturdy yet handsome shelving. Refined, badass, practical. Much like the ideals they promote.

The Real Deal continues with Contreras at the helm, the perfect place for this multitalented wonder woman. Many women who were mentored by Combs now work side-by-side in the Real Deal booth, teaching people of all ages the basics of practical (and fun) trades.

AMANDA ZITO

AMANDA ZITO SHOWED ARTISTIC TALENT FROM a young age, which developed into a unique style rooted in her early experiences growing up on her family's Montana ranch. With pointers from her older brother, she practiced techniques like value and the rule of thirds in primary school, seemingly preparing for her time at the Pacific Northwest College of Art.

For Amanda 2010 marked the beginning of a wild adventure in art, community, and motorcycles. She left Montana and headed west to Portland, Oregon, to attend PNCA, where she finished four years later with a bachelor of fine arts degree in illustration as well as a tattoo apprenticeship.

Experiencing homesickness and pining for Big Sky country, the ranch life, and the horses she grew up riding, Amanda decided to explore the world of motorcycles as an outlet. She spent the first two years riding mostly solo with her trusty 1980 Suzuki GS850 named "Lazarus." Traveling back and forth between Portland and home bimonthly, the motorcycle caused a shift in her road-trip approach. Jamming through 500 miles at a time on a motorcycle is much more tiring than it is on four wheels and encourages the rider to enjoy the sights, take the scenic route, and stretch their legs at viewpoints. Amanda felt that this, combined with an intimate connection with a temperamental carbureted machine, helped her feel less lonely on the road. She and Lazarus were making the trips *together*.

Amanda's incredible illustrations are released under the name "Blind Thistle," while her "As the Magpie Flies" moniker documents her motorcycle adventures on her website and social media channels. Her art has rapidly gained notice in the motorcycle industry, notably representing events, organizations, and businesses such as the MotoLady Women's Motorcycle Show (since 2016), the Dream Roll women's motorcycle campout, PNW Dual Sport, and Latus Motors Harley-Davidson in Gladstone, Oregon.

133

INCREDIBLE BUILDER AND HUMAN J. SHIA IS A mechanic and fabricator from Boston, Massachusetts. Not only does she create radical motorcycles, but she also fabricates many individual pieces of the bikes as if each is a tiny work of art. Which, really, they are. From using saxophones as exhaust pipes to chopping down shocks for coil mounts, J has a knack for details that make her builds very unique. She's garnered attention from most every motorcycle publication, has been featured on countless social media pages, and guest-judged custom bike shows alongside huge names like Craig Rodsmith.

135

One would think that she was born with a wrench in her hand, with a passion for motorcycles and mechanics. But, in fact, she sort of stumbled into building bikes, finding the love later. J comes from a long line of metalworkers and tinsmiths—more than a hundred years of them. Her family moved to the United States from Lebanon and Syria, bringing their tools and skills with them. They opened a restaurant and an auto shop, unknowingly laying the groundwork for J. Her family's house was known as the madhouse in the neighborhood—not only was her father a hoarder of things like washers and dryers, but they also had over seventy motorcycles in their yard. Her blue-collar family valued the idea of fixing things

rather than replacing them. "We fix everything," she says. "If the dishwasher breaks, we fix the dishwasher. Porch falls down, we fix the porch. As I was growing up, sometimes they'd fix things and then be able to sell them. So that turned into the motorcycle thing." Basically, a means to an end.

When she was fifteen, she got one of the yard bikes running and turned a profit on the sale. It became apparent that she had a pile of parts to pull from to make running bikes—and make ends meet. It wasn't always easy. "I frankly was a really shitty mechanic for the first five or six years," she admits. "All my customers were patient with me, but, you know, I just didn't know what I was doing. Over time I got all these lessons and became a better mechanic. It wasn't all easy, inherent, or natural to do it correctly, but it was natural to try to do it."

With determination comes reward. A way to make money when she couldn't find another job grew into a love for making rolling works of art. "It was just a way for me to pay my bills, it definitely wasn't an occupation I wanted to have," J says. "I wanted to be a traveling photographer, a war photographer." She's been able to combine her degree in fine art with her experience working on motorcycles. And the rolling works of art she builds with century-old tools from her family are something that resonates through the motorcycle industry.

GINGER McCABE

IF YOU'VE BEEN TO ANY MAJOR MOTORCYCLE show in the United States, you can bet you've seen Ginger McCabe's work. Her New Church Moto is an innovative custom motorcycle-seat company based in Oregon. A lover of unconventional designs, she favors commissions that require flexing strong creative muscles. She's made everything from tiny motorcycle seat–shaped trophies for the infamous One Motorcycle Show to classically styled seats.

You could say Ginger's art is inspired by her past. She was born in McCall, Idaho, to a mountain-loving family up to their elbows in creativity. Her love of sewing began in her father's shop, Long Valley Canvas, where he made bags, tents, awnings, and boat covers. Ginger recalls, "I can still smell the rolls of canvas and sewing machine oil, and hear the hum of industrial machines. I was just a tiny tot when he started the shop, but I spent many hours there, getting into trouble and sleeping under the machines. I'll always remember those times."

Growing up, Ginger worked with a wide array of fabrics, making everything from lingerie and wedding dresses to heavy-duty bags. In 2009 she landed a job at the historic Langlitz Leathers in Portland, Oregon. There she made jackets and other motorcycle gear, getting comfortable with leatherwork, which led to freelance gigs making motorcycle seats for friends. Just two years later, Ginger set off to work for herself and jumped into custom projects full time. New Church Moto was born!

Today some of the best-known bike builds feature Ginger's expert handiwork. She's busier than ever, living in the country where she feels most at home, with a hand-built mobile workshop she can tow wherever she's needed. Like many women who ride, she can often be found somewhere on the road.

AMY MULLIGAN

"DO NOT LET *anyone* TELL YOU WHAT YOU CAN AND CANNOT DO."

That's Amy Mulligan's number one piece of advice for motorcyclists, especially ladies. That indomitable attitude is no doubt what helped her become an aircraft mechanic and motorcycle builder before she was thirty. And not just any motorcycles, but crazy-looking rat bikes born of parts scrounged from collections of dead vehicles on her desert property in Tehachapi, California.

Amy started getting dirty in the desert dust when her cousin put her on a 110cc when she was seven. (It was a different time.) Her affinity for dirt riding continued to grow, as did her love for all things gas-guzzling. She started building custom cars at a local shop when she got older. Then the owner headed out of state, leaving her with nowhere to get greasy. Knowing her skill set and experience, a customer of the shop got her a job building airplanes. Yep, you heard that right. By day, Amy is an aircraft mechanic and composite technician. "I build and maintain experimental aircraft at scaled composites," she explains. When prodded for more, she says that, no, she doesn't work on UFOs, but literally shapes the bodywork out of carbon fiber and resin. On other days she'll pull a jet engine, build a hydraulic system, you know . . . no big.

When your everyday life involves bringing an engineer's aerospace designs to reality, building a motorcycle probably seems a bit more straightforward. Amy's thought was, "If I can build a car or an aircraft, why not a bike?" The foray into street riding started with her husband's 1982 BMW GS650, which she promptly crashed. Not easily deterred, she found herself determined to master everything motorcycle. Many miles and track days followed before a bike in buckets found its way to their home. The Suzuki GS450 was not all there—figuratively or literally—so Amy had to get a little creative. From the carcasses of a Kawasaki, Yamaha, BSA, and Chevy, "Mrs. Frankenstein" was born. The inaugural ride on "Frankie" is still one of Mulligan's most memorable experiences. The haphazard motorcycle might seem to some like it's having an identity crisis, but that's also what gives it so much charm. Frankie and Amy took home the People's Choice Award at the Women's Motorcycle Show in 2017. Since then, another weird-yet-wonderful bike has been added to the build list: a GS750 named "Uncle Fester." No doubt we'll be seeing more wild stuff from this creative lass in the coming years—perhaps even second iterations of Frankie and Fester.

"As rat bikes, these bikes are never really done being built," Amy says. "They will change as I ride them and find stuff I like and don't like. That's the most interesting part: they are an unending extension of you."

143

KRYSTAL HESS

LIFE CAN SOMETIMES LEAVE US FEELING LIKE A boat with no rudder, but it's where you land after everything goes sideways that really counts. Krystal Hess is a shining example, but it wasn't easy. The long, tough process she went through led her to create Motorcycle Missions, a nonprofit dedicated to helping veterans and first responders with PTSD through motorcycle therapy.

Krystal grew up in the great white north—Calgary, Alberta, to be exact. Her love for custom vehicles started with her first car, a Ford Probe with a chameleon paint job, which sparked her interest in mechanics. She tried to get local auto shops to let her intern and get some hands-on experience, but no one took her up on it. "Everybody thought I was crazy, but it was a passion of mine," she told Loryn Cole, creator of the popular moto website Ridewell. Later, after becoming a nurse and getting married, life took a turn. Marital bliss was not that at all, and Hess ended her abusive relationship. Motorcycles weren't on her radar until postdivorce, when she was dreaming of ways to start over. She had her sights set on sunny So-Cal, but after meeting a custom motorcycle builder who lived in Austin, she found herself moving to big ol' Texas. It's not the West Coast, but it's definitely sunny and has an amazing motorcycle community.

Though she hadn't yet learned to ride, Krystal and her beau took on a custom motorcycle project together, tearing down a Hayabusa and refinishing the parts. Krystal learned to powder coat, turning the bright orange bike into candy blue. The bike was back together as a rolling chassis when her world was turned upside down again. During a bipolar episode, her boyfriend dismantled the motorcycle and attempted suicide. In the aftermath of the tragic events, Krystal found herself strapped for cash with a garage full of tools and a pile of parts. While offloading some of her tools, she met a mechanic who inquired about the

145

Hayabusa project. One thing led to another and she found herself working with him to reassemble the bike, learning as she went. After a summer working in the shop at the dealership reassembling the bike, she realized it had been a transformative process. "Getting to that point was just a sigh of relief," she explains. She had found her calling.

With her newfound realization that building bikes was the best therapy she had found, Krystal started working at the dealership where she rebuilt the 'Busa. They carved out an area in the shop for her to work on projects and in the next year she built six motorcycles, one of which was a Suzuki Savage café racer named "Spinderella" that was featured on the MotoLady website as a contest winner in 2013. The black and pink bike features historic photos of moto ladies plastered on the bodywork and was "built in honor of all the badass femme-fatale riders everywhere. It is an homage to women—past, present, and future—who love to ride." This first introduction to Krystal, learning she had powder-coated all the pink bits herself, was very memorable. Spinderella was just the first of many award-winning custom motorcycles built under Krystal's business, Ricochet Customs, including an Indian Scout and a Forty Creek Whiskey commission. The retro-looking Yamaha bobber took

home three first-place trophies in the first six months of showing, including People's Choice in the J&P Cycles Ultimate Builder Custom Bike Show at Dallas in 2015.

Motorcycle Missions started in 2017 when Krystal realized she had the tools, literally, to help veterans she had met at local bike nights who were dealing with post-traumatic stress disorder. After becoming friends with a lot of the folks, she realized there was a connection between her work as a nurse, helping people, and her love of custom bikes. The first Motorcycle Missions build was revealed at the Republic of Texas Biker Rally and received loads of positive feedback. An experiment quickly snowballed in the best way possible, and the team was starting (and finishing) new projects left and right. She found that having a goal-oriented activity to focus on, with clear milestones, can be a great coping mechanism. The motorcycle community itself lends to healing with its closeness. The finished custom motorcycles find homes touring in shows and are raffled off for charity. And veterans and first responders get to build something with a team. "They've accomplished a mission, and they've done it with brothers and sisters, just like on the battlefield," Krystal says.

LANAKILA MᴄNAUGHTON

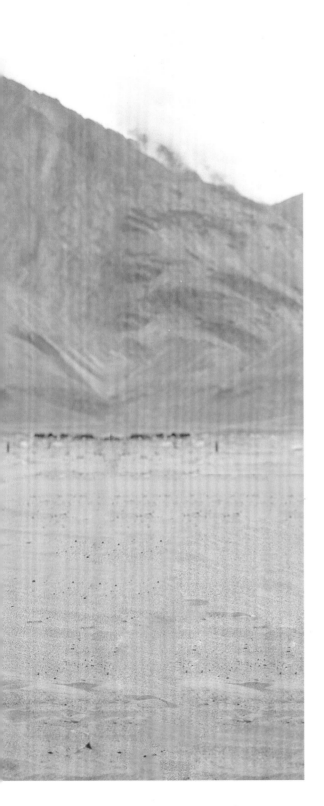

LANAKILA MACNAUGHTON'S WORK IS PREVALENT in the world of motorcycling. With its striking contrasts and extra crisp composition, it's no wonder why.

Smashing into the two-wheel world less than a decade ago, Lana's work quickly spread through reposts on social media sites such as Tumblr and Instagram. As her popularity grew, so did her travel opportunities. Since starting the Women's Moto Exhibit, a traveling photo gallery documenting the new wave of women motorcyclists, she's photographed hundreds of women riders. She's worked with brands like Google and Harley-Davidson, and she's had her work featured in *The Oprah Magazine*. She's captured images in locations including Dubai, Kenya, and Tanzania.

As a sophomore outside Portland, Oregon, Lana found herself less than enthused with high school life. Signing up for a photography class so she and her friends could hang out rather than hit the books, she stumbled into a new passion. After learning the ins and outs of the darkroom, she moved on to a bigger, badder Holga medium-format film camera. "I would take terrible photos," she claims, explaining that her camera went everywhere with her. "I started shooting [medium format], doing multiple exposures, and just kept taking photos."

After a trip to See See Motor Coffee in Portland, things shifted gears. She already loved Americana, history, vintage bikes, and motorcycle culture. "I didn't know this whole world existed, and I was just so inspired," she recalls. "That really opened my eyes." About six months later she had saved up enough money to get herself a starter bike: a little 1982 Honda 250 purchased for $700. They were inseparable. "I rode it evvvvverywhere," she says. "In rain, snow . . . any excuse to ride, I would take the bike. It squealed when I turned it on, it was red, I loved it."

That's how both the Women's Moto Exhibit and The Dream Roll ladies camping trip came to be. "When

149

I got my motorcycle I wanted to get women from the community together to ride motorcycles with. It was really hard to find women, ya know, ten years ago. I met women like Stormie Ray who have so much confidence and are so fun. Women I look up to."

Lanakila noticed a lack of media featuring women riders. "For some reason, it became really important to me to document women I meet for future generations," she explains. "Women on motorcycles aren't represented for what seems like a very long time. I want to capture these women and tell their stories. Women in a hundred years, who knows how free they're going to be. Technology is just taking over, and my motorcycle is one of the best ways for me to feel better. I hope these photos inspire those women, my grandchildren, or whatever, to not be indoctrinated by our culture and do whatever makes them happy."

One of the rad ladies she encountered through her work, Becky Goebel, has become her partner in the Dream Roll, a women's motorcycle camping weekend that takes place in the Pacific Northwest each year near the beginning of summer. Becky, who was living in Vancouver, Canada, and Lana had only met a couple of times when they decided to start the event. "I just wanted to make a really cool, inclusive

camping trip for women who ride. I didn't really know what to expect, but it's a million times better than I ever could have imagined it. The type of women who come—it's really special to me. It's probably the one time a year when I feel so connected, wild, and free. That's the spirit of Dream Roll; everyone puts on that vibe and energy when they show up."

These days Lanakila's focusing a little less on the motorcycle industry, having started a new business in Boise, Idaho, that will separate her bread and butter from her passion. But she won't stop shooting women riders. "I think I'll always continue to do it. Try to diversify, shoot more women of color, trans women,

and share more stories," she explains. Right now she's running her business and training for the Build/Train/ Race series on her custom flat-track bike built by Sean Smith. The Royal Enfield series, masterminded by another awesome woman, Bree Poland, started in 2020 as a part of the American Flat Track (AFT) program. Three other women—Melissa Paris (pro racer), Jillian Deschenes (motorcycle enthusiast), and Andrea Lothrop (DIY shop owner)—competed on their customized Royal Enfield INT650 twins.

152

BLACK GIRLS Ride

MORE THAN A MAGAZINE....
ITS A **MOVEMENT**!

Vol 4. JUNE 2011
JOIN THE MOVEMENT

HAWG DIVAS
RIDING INTO THE
21ST CENTURY

RACER REPORT
MIROCK WRAP UP
WITH ERIKA ALLISON

GEARED UP
5 BOOTS TO HELP
YOU KICK UP DUST

PETEY VEE
COMMITTED TO WINNING

WWW.BLACKGIRLSRIDE.COM
MOTORCYCLES • ACCESSORIES • EVENTS • FASHION

THE
COMMITMENT
MARCH
"GET YOUR KNEE OFF OUR NECKS"
AUGUST 28th, 2020   WASHINGTON, D.C.

Boss lady Porsche Taylor didn't grow up on a bike, but that doesn't mean she's any less enthusiastic. Quite the opposite. Porsche is the founder of *Black Girls Ride*, a website, magazine, and network featuring informative articles, community forums, and photo galleries. A native of Los Angeles, she got her bachelor's degree at the University of California before going on to an internship at Virgin Records, followed by A&M. Later she went on to become the entertainment marketing manager at Adidas. In January 2011 she founded *Black Girls Ride*. (Fun fact, that was the same time as MotoLady!)

What is *Black Girls Ride*? It's "the first-ever motorcycle magazine in celebration of women of color." It's a movement and a message—one of inclusion, celebrating all women who ride. In Porsche's words, it's "not an exclusive racial statement; rather, it's an inclusive celebration of all women who live to ride. It's the positive, fearless, unapologetic, take-charge attitude we exhibit on these machines." It's about sharing joy on the open road.

The idea came about when Porsche was researching the history of black women motorcyclists and found the legendary Bessie Stringfield. Bessie rode across America, solo, when she was eighteen—in the 1930s. As one of the first women dispatch riders for the U.S. military, Bessie has an impressive legacy. Her story, and others, were ones that Porsche wanted to share with the world. "As a community, our history tends to be more oral than written. This meant that rider profiles on women of color were very hard to find," she notes.

With a decade of growing the connection of her community under her belt, it's clear she's done exactly what she set out to do.

YOU MAY KNOW HER AS THE "ROADRASH QUEEN" or "Queen Bee." Brittany Morrow has made it a life goal to instill the importance of motorcycle gear on riders around the planet. And for good reason. At twenty years old, Brittany's life got flipped upside down when she was thrown from the back of her friend's motorcycle at 120 mph. Wearing a borrowed helmet that was too big and no other protective gear, she was basically skinned alive when she hit the ground. She violently tumbled and slid down the asphalt, quite sure she was about to be a goner, for a total of 522 feet. Morrow was carted off to the hospital forty-five minutes later, facing a long and painful recovery process. With

more than 50 percent of her body needing full-thickness skin grafts, Brittany says, "It took the doctors two months, three blood transfusions, thirty-one dressing changes, and nine surgeries to put Humpty Dumpty back together again."

Did this brush with death scare her away from riding? *Nope.* It was only nine months before she took the training courses, bought her own motorcycle (and head-to-toe safety gear), and started riding on her own. Forever changed, she knew she had the strength to get through pretty much anything that might come her way. With this newfound perspective and appreciation for the simple things, she came to accept her scars and connect with people. "I thought looking the way I

did would further alienate me, but instead, it opened a door; riders began asking me about my scars and I had the opportunity to share my story with many people."

In 2006 the full account of her experience hit the internet and went viral. "I learned that motorcycle safety was an attitude and a choice that I had to make every time I went riding," Brittany says. "However, the most important thing I came to realize was that these lessons were not meant for me alone. I was newly and uniquely made to share what I had learned with the world."

An avid track rider and road racer, Brittany has spent the last fifteen years honing her craft and sharing her story. She's worked as a professional instructor since

2009, and her work as a Motorcycle Safety Foundation RiderCoach in Basic, Experienced, Advanced, and Military Sportbike has given her opportunities to train motorcyclists hands on. In addition, she was certified as an instructor for Total Control Training, working on the California Motorcyclist Safety Program until 2017. Her keynote talks have taken her far and wide to conferences, rallies, and bike shows to speak on the importance of safety. Yes, motorcycling is dangerous, but with protection and training, it can be an amazingly fun way to travel, commute, or even just go fast. The Roadrash Queen is living proof.

LORYN COLE, PREVIOUSLY LORYN THOMPSON, is a Texas transplant living in the Pacific Northwest. Born in Austin, she grew up in Dripping Springs, west of Austin in beautiful Hill Country. Her love for writing, eye for design, and education in marketing all led her to create an awesome resource for motorcycle enthusiasts who want to be safe. Loryn's warm personality made her an effective educator, and her calculated approach to motorcycling and mechanics made her an awesome builder.

After graduating from the University of North Texas, she moved to Dallas with her boyfriend. One day he decided to check out a motorcycle dealership. As often happens in the world of motorcycling, they were swept up by the idea and suddenly found themselves sitting in the financing office. Loryn, being more analytical about things, was wide-eyed and eager to reassess the situation. "That fiasco led us to taking

the motorcycle class together in November of 2013," she recalls. "I remember it was November because a freak ice storm came through and the class got cut short." With the lack of seat time, she still wasn't sure about committing to a full-size bike and picked up a scooter. She zipped around on all 150cc for a year before wanting something bigger and more eye-catching like her boyfriend's Royal Enfield. And that's how she ended up with the Little Rat, her custom GT-Moto-built Kawasaki café racer. "It was a piece of crap when I bought it, totally not worth what I paid for it," she says. "It was very embarrassing." A story so many of us find relatable.

Shortly after picking up the KZ, her boyfriend had a rattling motorcycle crash that made her examine all sides of riding. She had to reflect and see if it was something she wanted to continue. "I don't think a lot of riders have that experience. Not that I want

more motorcyclists to crash—obviously not, but I do wish more of them would have that first-hand experience to help them. I feel like there's this kind of old motorcycle culture of being safe is not cool, being safe is not fun. But I think there are people like me that don't see the conflict between having fun and wearing a helmet, having fun and wearing quality boots. So it can still be fun when you're wearing gear. That was really the impetus for starting to do my research about being a safe rider and starting to find gear that was certified to be safe, which not a lot of it is."

Loryn started Ridewell in the fall of 2014, after purchasing the bike. This is when she connected with Sofi Tsingos of GT-Moto who agreed to take on the custom café project. She wanted to take advantage of the rebuild time to get her bike knowledge up to speed. Upon doing research, Loryn realized that the information she wanted was either difficult to find,

totally unclear, or didn't exist. With the lack of ability to find safe gear, and an overall lack of industry representation for riders who both like to go fast and be safe, plus her long-time love of writing, Ridewell was born. Since its creation, her website has flourished with informative articles about everything from riding tips to gear reviews. On top of that, she didn't settle for riding a beautiful bike built by a badass woman. She wanted to build her own, taking on the Ridewell Rebuild—a Honda XL250 from the ground up. She pulled out all the stops, taking a Portland Community College metal shop class where she learned to weld and do basic metal shaping. The finished bike, a total stunner, was featured with the Little Rat in the tenth anniversary of Portland's One Motorcycle Show.

ANYA VIOLET AGHABABIAN AND ASHMORE ELLIS may not have realized when they got a group of gals together for a motorcycle campout that they would be starting a movement. The 2013 get-together, dubbed "Babes in Borrego," took lady motorcyclists through the beautiful, sweeping roads of the Southern California Anza-Borrego Desert and ended at a Borrego Springs, where fifty badass babes slept under the stars. Born from a simple idea to introduce women riders to each other, the event quickly grew into a massive get-together drawing women from across the world. "We wanted to meet more women who ride," they explain. "We never planned on it becoming an event series. We just wanted to go camping and make some new friends."

For 2014 the event morphed into Babes Ride Out. It had a whole new look and a whole new location. "All the women who came to the first campout were so fun and enthusiastic," Aghababian and Ellis recall. "It was their energy and encouragement that inspired us to keep it going." A wave of moto babes crashed through the Joshua Tree Desert—more than six hundred of them. In the years that followed the inaugural campout, thousands of women have trekked from as far as Australia to attend the unique women's-only event. During the day they encourage everyone to leave the campsite and get out to ride, providing maps and guided group rides. At night the party starts. If you want to drink and dance, they've got bars hawking mixed drinks and incredible bands rocking the stage. If you want to get your learn on, they have vendors that include the Real Deal women, with workshops on welding, pinstriping, leathercraft, and even jewelry making.

While the idea of a women's-only event can strike some the wrong way, its effect is great. The idea of a father and son in the garage is almost timeless at this point—as a man, you're supposed to know how

to change a tire, check your oil—the basics. But for the longest time, many women were not treated that same way. The ones who were handed a wrench as a kid have become incredible forces in the industry—ladies like Sofi Tsingos and J. Shia. The rest of us have a passion for motorcycling but might sometimes feel overmatched riding into a group of guys, feeling like all eyes are on us, and if we mess up it's the end of the world. That is exactly where events like BRO come in. They allow women of all ages and backgrounds to come together with no judgment and exchange or gain experiences. If you drop your bike, five chicks immediately appear around you to help. Then you ride off as if nothing happened.

"No dudes, no 'tudes." That's the BRO motto.

SELF-PROCLAIMED "MAKER OF *MAD MAX* WASTELAND machines," motorcycle mechanic Olivia Montalbano hails from Northern California near Sacramento. Not only is she one with a wrench when it comes to repairs, but she also likes to tear apart beat-up bikes and breathe new life into their rattly bones with postapocalyptic treatments. Her excitement for what she does has spread to tens of thousands of YouTube followers, and even her mom, whom she taught how to ride.

She bought her first bike in 2014, a little Kawasaki Ninja, and learned how to ride. The following year she found herself wanting something with a little more power and upgraded to a 2001 Suzuki Bandit 1200. Due to a leaky petcock, which seemed like a simple enough fix to take on herself, she cracked into the mechanics for the first time. The next year she bought herself a Harley Sportster and found out it needed a lot more work than expected. Suddenly she was spending nights in the garage learning how to work on each project as she went. The more she fixed stuff, the more she loved the process. She and the Harley had a torrid love affair that took her all up and down the West Coast to

motorcycle events like Babes Ride Out in Joshua Tree, California. She had found her calling.

Hot on the heels of her newfound passion, she spent 2017 bothering local motorcycle shops to see if anyone needed a hand. While she heard "no" time and time again, she did get some advice: "Just keep trying. And don't go to school, you'll just get in a lot of debt. Find someone to take you on as an apprentice."

This led Olivia to Vintage Monkey, a restoration shop (and so much more) owned and founded by Shasta Smith, where she worked for a year. In the following years she worked her way up from hawking bits and pieces at a parts store to working in the service department at a dealership. She's since built multiple custom bikes, some of which have been featured at the Women's Motorcycle Show and on MAVTV's *Wrench Wars*.

Olivia says if there's anything to take away from her story, it's don't give up. With hard work and dedication, she became a motorcycle mechanic in two years and with no school. All because she wanted to do what she loved.

PINK

DID YOU KNOW PROLIFIC POP ARTIST PINK, GIVEN name Alecia Beth Moore, is also a motorcyclist? Not only have motorcycles appeared in her music videos and photoshoots, but they are also a part of her at-home life. She and former pro motocross racer Carey Hart met in 2001 when he was competing in the X Games and have been married since 2006. Their whole family, including two little ones, are on two wheels, including dirt bikes and Alecia and Carey's collection of streetbikes that ranges from choppers to modified Indian Scout cruisers. Carey even built her a custom Indian Chieftain featuring Rosie the Riveter on the rear fender for her "push present" (basically a thank-you gift from the father for going through

labor). She posed with the bike for a photo on social media, saying, "I give you babies and you build me motorcycles. Some girls like diamonds, I like heavy metal and carbon-fiber and chrome."

Growing up, Pink was both creative and competitive. Between four and twelve she was a gymnast, and in high school she joined her first band. Shortly after, she got her start in the music business. At fourteen she was performing at clubs in Philadelphia, where she officially became Pink. (It should be noted this moniker was adopted from *Reservoir Dogs* character Mr. Pink, who's a bit wily and incredibly intelligent.) At sixteen she started playing in a three-girl group called Choice. Their work caught the eye of Antonio

Marquis "L.A." Reid at Atlanta's La Face Records, and they were signed shortly after. Although they recorded an album that was never released, their song "Key to My Heart" was included in the 1996 film *Kazaam*. Reid wanted to continue working with Pink, but not with Choice, and the group disbanded in 1998. Two years later she released her first album, *Can't Take Me Home*, and it went double platinum. Though she had sold 15 million records, she found herself destitute due to bad deals. "I had been screwed, blued, and tattooed by every person I came across," she said in an interview with *Variety*. "It was a lot of lessons at a really young age, but I paid attention because I don't like to make the same mistake twice."

Her perseverance paid off. In the two decades since her solo debut, Pink has sold over 60 million albums and 75 million singles and has had fifteen singles in the top ten of the Billboard 100, with four at number one. She's received numerous accolades and awards, including three Grammys, seven MTV Video Music Awards, two MTV Europe Awards, three Billboard Music Awards, two People's Choice Awards, and a Daytime Emmy. Billboard named her Woman of the Year in 2013, and she was tenth in VH1's 100 Greatest Women in Music. She was honored with a Hollywood Star in 2019.

SUZY PILACZYNSKI

SOME FOLKS BUST INTO SCENES LIKE THE KOOL-Aid man smashes through walls, and that's how a lot of people felt when Suzy Pilaczynski brought her blue Harley Shovelhead "Hexaglide" to the Born Free Motorcycle Show in 2019. Perhaps unbeknownst to many, Suzy has been co-owner of Old-Stf Cycle Shop in Yuba City, California, with her husband for fifteen years. Although they specialize in manufacturing custom and replacement parts for bikes of the cruiser and chopper varieties, Suzy just never got around to getting her own motorcycle. The usual life stuff—time, money, distractions—all kept her from making that dream a reality.

While most new parents struggle to find time for new projects, the opposite was true for Suzy and her husband when they added a daughter to their clan. Their little one was a big motivator to build a bike, and Born Free's People's Champ category gave her the last push. She threw her hat in the ring and said, "Well, shit, I guess I'm finally building my bike . . . I'll figure out how to do it as I go." And boy howdy did she do just that. Inspired by art deco and bold colors of the '70s and '80s, she collected ideas from usual and unusual places, like vintage bikes, fashion, and home hardware. She even taught herself 3D CAD and used the software to help bring her vision to

life. Right before the show, she was still putting the finishing touches on the beautiful 1977 "Hexaglide" that ended up winning her the Born Free trophy. Seeing this bike in person is mesmerizing. All the details run together, and the more you look, the better it gets. Hexagon-shaped forks, matching fuel lines, a wild heim-joint top motor mount—it's no wonder she became the first solo woman to score a win at Born Free, and subsequently, the first to be an officially invited builder.

When asked, "Why choppers?" Suzy has a great reply. "Well, my Miss America answer would be because they're a symbol of freedom, rebellion,

exploration," she says. "But honestly, I never really stopped to think about it. I'm an extremely inquisitive, artistic person who loves a challenge, and motorcycles seemed to be a natural fit. Building a bike lets me use my analytical side to pick it apart, observe how everything works, and devise new or different ways of accomplishing the same thing. Meanwhile, my creative side gets to figure out how to transform it into something aesthetically pleasing, while still being functional. I feel like you really need both sides in order to make it cohesive and eye catching."

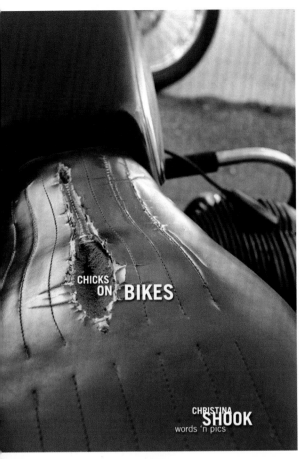

CHRISTINA SHOOK, TO ME, IS A PIONEER IN THE world of women in motorcycling media. Published in 2009, her book *Chicks on Bikes* was one of the first to take an in-depth look at real women riders from all walks of life. Her work inspires deeper thought on the realm of motorcycling beyond gender and occupation. What drives you? What makes you ride? How have motorcycles changed your way of life? All are questions silently posed in her book—and answered with her photographic exploration of all types of lady riders.

Christina earned a master of fine arts degree from the San Francisco Art Institute. As a journalism major, she quickly realized that she much preferred the photographic side of the work. Originally from the Midwest, she wanted to cultivate more relationships with women after moving to the Bay Area. Combining that objective with her love of riding and passion for photography proved successful, leading not just to *Chicks on Bikes* but also to an ongoing project capturing real women who ride.

Most inspired by the grit of tenacious explorers like Effie and Avis Hotchkiss, the first women to ride cross-country on motorcycles in 1915, Christina evokes the same spirit with her work. Her own deep love for two wheels began more than twenty-five years ago with her first motorcycle, a beat-up Honda Nighthawk that often needed to be bump-started coasting down the hill outside her San Francisco home. Her bike collection has since included everything from a 1979 BMW R100S to a Ducati ST4.

When asked whether she considers herself a role model, Christina responds, "Only in my avid support for all women motorcyclists to come together and promote the joy and freedom of riding as acceptable for all women. I think that the support of one another is vital."

Amen to that, Christina.

169

PAIGE MACY

PAIGE MACY'S SAVVY WITH A SPRAY GUN IS AS intense as her paint jobs. In a few short years, she's gone from getting tips about automotive paint from friends at shops to executing intricate '70s-style paint jobs that play tricks on your eyes. Her bikes are layered with metalflake, kandies, and stripes of all kinds, so it's only appropriate that her company is called Stripe Cult Painting.

Originally from the Northwest Territories in Canada, Paige and her family moved to Salt Lake City when she was eight. After high school, Paige attended the Art Institute of Salt Lake City, where her mom had taught on and off for four years. Not satisfied at art school, Paige found herself switching majors multiple times before eventually realizing that she didn't want to sit in a classroom. Watching presentations about art and design wasn't her speed. She wanted to paint, draw, create—and make a living off it.

For a year Paige worked as a tattoo apprentice before things fizzled out. Then for a while she worked as a server, painting in her spare time. Then things took a turn in 2016, and life slowly began pointing her in the direction of her calling. After hands-on paint lessons with friends, the painting fever took over. Paige soon found herself a mentor, Kim, at an auto body shop in Utah. It didn't take long to get going on the intricate, flashy paint jobs she had been drawn to. Now she's self-employed, giving helmets and motorcycles custom makeovers and working as the in-house painter for Salt City Builds.

As for getting her own bike, it just sort of just happened for Paige. The desire had been there for a long time, but the stars aligned when her friend Rev from Salt City Builds proposed building her a bike with her tax return money—a KZ650 café racer. But pretty quickly Paige had her eye on something bigger that spoke to her personal style. She wanted a chopper. "I wanted my bike to be pointy and have sharp edges," she explains. "I didn't want it to look like anyone else's and I wanted it to fit my personality." So a Sportster 1200 was reworked from the ground up, designed by Paige, fabricated by Salt City Builds, and finished with a gorgeous Stripe Cult paint job.

JESSIE GENTRY

JESSIE GENTRY IS A PHOTOGRAPHER FROM Los Angeles who studied photography and fine art at the prestigious ArtCenter College of Design in Pasadena. This experience refined her love for creating beautiful imagery and allowed her to hone her craft. Her works often highlight strong, talented women who build up each other and are shown in their element. Capturing their style within the mood of the images themselves, she evokes movement even in her static scenes.

She now works with brands like Stellar Moto Brand (specializing in unique protective gear for women who ride), Mattel, and Vinyl Cosmetics (a high quality, cruelty-free makeup line founded by lady rider Sheena Walker). Jessie also cofounded the Velvets MC, an all-female motorcycle group that hosts charity events and donates proceeds to Planned Parenthood and other nonprofits. One of the most notable events had to be the Velvets Rodeo, where they brought a mechanical bull inside a motorcycle shop and let all the liquored-up attendees have a go at eight seconds.

Gentry also is a talented writer and has been published in print in *Motorcyclist* magazine, and on websites such as RideApart. These days you can find her living in Bend, Oregon, on a ranch with her sister, Katie. She welcomes the change of scenery, and the pair have a small collection of goats, pigs, chickens, ducks, and even bees.

STACIE B. LONDON

STACIE B. LONDON IS A LOS ANGELES–BASED industrial designer with a master's degree from ArtCenter College of Design in Pasadena. Her fascination with motorcycles and all things fast and free runs in her blood. In fact, her father set a land-speed record in Bonneville in 1965, starting the obsession before she was even born.

As a third-generation Angelena, being around muscle cars and powerboats was the norm. Growing up with American-made V-8s and spending summers in the Pacific Ocean, she quickly grew accustomed to the wind in her face. As a child, she decided that she

needed a motorcycle, but it took a while to fulfill that dream. In May 2009 she finally purchased her first bike, a 1969 BMW R60US. What a place to start!

Long involved in the arts, personally and professionally, she works at the Museum of Contemporary Art (MOCA) in Los Angeles as the exhibition designer and has had the privilege of managing the mechanical restoration and operation of one of Chris Burden's seminal artworks. *The Big Wheel* is a kinetic sculpture in which Burden brilliantly brings together a 1968 Ward's Riverside (Benelli) 250cc motorcycle and an 1800s, eight-

foot-diameter cast iron flywheel. *The Big Wheel* also brought together Stacie's interest in technology, performance, art, and adventure.

Stacie is also the founder and president of the East Side Moto Babes, a women's motorcycle group in Los Angeles that is interested in developing a sisterhood among women and in expanding their motorcycling skills on and off the road. Weeknights she hosts group rides around LA proper, and many weekends you'll find her out racing her vintage bikes under the team name Triple Nickel 555. One of her first racing seasons was quite the challenge, when she

rode a 1968 Honda CB160 with the American Historic Racing Motorcycle Association (AHRMA) and Chuckwalla Valley Motorcycle Association (CVMA). In 2015 the AHRMA named her the Female Road Racer of the Year. She became a Southern California Timing Association (SCTA) land-speed record holder when one of her runs in 2018 at El Mirage clocked her at 97.538 mph in the 250/M-PF class on a Harley-Davidson Aermacchi Sprint.

GEVIN FAX & TANA ROLLER

APPEARING AT MOTO EVENTS ACROSS AMERICA with smiling faces and the most upbeat attitudes, Gevin Fax and Tana Roller are the embodiment of all the good things within the motorcycling community.

Gevin is an actor, teacher, musician, and athlete. At a young age she found success in both athletics and music. After high school her team took second in the 1983 USSSA Women's Slow Pitch World Nationals, and she played basketball at High State University in North Carolina where they were first in the region and state.

On top of that, Gevin was signed to the MCA record label in 1991 as bassist with the band KLYMAXX. Their album *The Maxx Is Back* reached No. 32 on the *Billboard* charts. "I guess I just have a lot of dreams," she said through a laugh.

As for her lifelong love affair with motorcycles, Gevin's pops put her on a minibike at about eight. By thirteen she was on a 90cc Bridgestone with a clutch. She's done well over one million miles in her five-something decades on two wheels. Breaking the mold as a supertalented, ultraindependent motorcycling woman, Gevin was a two-time cover girl for some of the first women's motorcycling publications. "I was only ever wanted for women's mags because men wouldn't touch me with a 10-foot pole since I'm black," she explained. Their obviously antiquated opinions proved idiotic when she became one of four riders in the popular Discovery Network documentary, *Biker Women* in 1996, starring alongside Jamie Elvidge (one of the first female pro motorcycle journalists), Cris Sommer-Simmons (founder of the first magazine for women motorcyclists, *Harley Women*, and author of *The American Motorcycle Girls: 1900–1950*), and Gail DeMarco (author of *Rebels with a Cause: We Ride the Harley*).

While the style of Gevin's rides haven't changed much (one of her favorites has done half or more of those million miles), she found herself searching for a new type of event, a new group. "The old Harley crowd is just a dying breed right now. I might have come out of that breed, but I'm going to move forward." Gevin turned to social media. It put her in touch with other women who look forward to cultivating a positive community. "I love popping into your world. It's like, oh my god, I found my people!"

Tana, another multitalented force to be reckoned with, grew up on a motorcycle and explored many different outlets for her creative proclivities. She found success in film/TV, casting, and hair styling ("anything hands-on"). "According to my Dad, I rolled out of the womb on a motorcycle," Tana said. "And he's the reason." Her first bike at just five years old was a 50cc Honda Monkey. Growing up in a motorcycle shop is a dream for little girls who have the need for speed, and early access to demo bikes and supercross tracks are the things about which some motorheads only get to fantasize.

Motorcycling was an important part of Tana's life, but her daughter wasn't a big fan. So she decided to take a break, "I was a single parent . . . I was the kind of mom to be like, that has to wait for me then. Long story short, later I started riding again, and I was looking for women." When she found Babes Ride Out on Instagram, she headed to the desert, just like that. "It was the first time I had packed a bike for the street, and I did it all wrong, but I made it safely. I met some phenomenal women that first time around. It was sort of a reawakening of my soul. I didn't realize what I was missing until I took that break."

In 2017 both Gevin and Tana attended a charity event called the Ride Against Femicide, which works to "help women escape domestic violence deaths one shelter at a time." The two hit it off and have been practically attached at the hip ever since. Shortly after meeting Gevin and her experience at Babes Ride Out, Tana found herself "wanting to do something with soul." Tana wondered, "What can we create out of this? We need a purpose. I was sitting with this group of girls, looked around and went, 'this is my wolfpack.' I needed to do something with it."

That's when A Quest Called Tribe was born. Having found her wolfpack, wild rides, and wellness, Tana wanted to connect the dots. In her fight against cancer, she came to believe the mental state has a lot to do with good health. Riding motorcycles and making these connections continues to play a huge part in her treatment. "The only name I could come up with for this thing was A Quest Called Tribe because that's what it was about to me. Who are these people that you want to spend your life with? It's ever-evolving." Upcoming documentaries will feature their life and adventures on the road, and delve into Tana's journey with cancer, motorcycles, and healing. The films will feature everything from those momentous moments on the road when everything is right to the less-glamorous, realistic side of motorcycling (eating at rest stops, staying healthy on the road, and other blunders of travel).

ALICIA MARIAH ELFVING IS THE FOUNDER OF TheMotoLady.com, often called the world's leading website for women who ride, and started the Women's Motorcycle Show, the world's first custom bike show featuring bikes built and raced by ladies. Elfving has been a journalist for a decade, and her photography has been featured in *Cosmopolitan* magazine, in national news broadcasts like *Good Morning America*, on the front page of Reddit, and across the homepages of Yahoo, AOL, and CNN. Her articles have appeared in *The Huffington Post*, *Motorcyclist* magazine, Motorcycle.com, Expedition Portal, and others. Two of her own custom motorcycle builds have been featured on the top moto sites BikeEXIF and Silodrome, the first being her custom 1998 Ducati Monster named "Pandora's Box." Championing women motorcyclists of all varieties, her work got her noticed by Gerber Gear in 2016 and led to her becoming one of their "badassadors" alongside Tim Kennedy, Bear Grylls, Jess Pryles, and other industry leaders.

A native to the super green, rainy lands of the Pacific Northwest, Alicia loved adventure from an early age. Whether it was camping with Mom or going mushroom hunting and fishing with her Dad, she was introduced to survival and preparedness from a young age. These hands-on skills were nurtured, growing her love for arts, crafts, and building things in general. The need to explore, create, and continue moving fuels her projects from leather craft to event coordination. Elfving insists she's not built to just sit still: "It feels like I start dying if I stay still too long, similar to a shark."

Elfving roams roadways far and wide looking for experiences and personalities to capture with her words and photographs. She splits her time between her hometown Portland, Oregon, and Los Angeles, California.

PHOTO CREDITS

A = all, **B** = bottom, **L** = left, **R** = right, **T** = top

• **TITLE PAGES:** Getty Images/Gunther/Keystone/ Hulton Archive, 2. • **TABLE OF CONTENTS:** Author photo, 4TL; David Boyd, 4BL; Jimmy Ban, 4BR; Lois Pryce, 5TL; Getty Images/Buda Mendes/LatinContent, 5TR; Getty Images/PAUL CROCK/AFP, 5BL; Getty Images/Mirrorpix, 5BR. • **INTRODUCTION:** Author photo, 6 –7; Brandon LaJoie, 8 –9; Cam Elkins, 10–11. • **HISTORY MAKERS:** Author photo, 12 –13. **Jessi Combs:** Corey Piehowicz, 14; Aaron Packard, 16L; Author photo, 16R. **Gloria Tramontin Struck:** Michael Lichter, 19. **Valerie Thompson:** Courtesy of rider, 22–23. **Hannah Johnson:** Courtesy of rider/ photo Dana Añar, 24. **Leslie Porterfield:** Alamy Stock Photo/Historic Collection, 25. Laia Sanz: Getty Images/ Dean Mouhtaropoulos, 26; Getty Images/Dan Istitene, 27. **Kate Johnston:** Courtesy of rider, 28–29. **Wendy Crockett:** Adam Fondren, 30; American Motorcyclist Association, 31. **Jenny Tinmouth:** Getty Images/ Ker Robertson, 32; Getty Images/Joe Giddens – PA Images, 33. **Beryl Swain:** Getty Images/Mirrorpix, 34– 35; Getty Images/Mirrorpix, 36–37A. **Maria Costello:** LAT Motorsports/Jeff Bloxham, 38–39. **Ana Carrasco Gabarrón:** Getty Images/Mirco Lazzari gp, 44; Getty Images/Jose Breton/NurPhoto, 45. **Taru Rinne:** Jarl Asklund, 46–47A. • **ADVENTURERS:** Courtesy of Lois Pryce, 48–49. **Lois Pryce:** Courtesy of rider, 50– 53. **Adeline & Augusta Van Buren:** Courtesy of Van Buren Family, 54–55 and 56–57B. **Alicia Sornosa:** Courtesy of rider, 58–59. Esha Gupta: Courtesy of rider/photos Ankit Gandhi, 60–61. Sherri **Jo Wilkins:** Walter Colebatch, 62–63; Courtesy of rider, 63. **Aileen Guenther:** Courtesy of rider, 64; Tofan Angga, 65. Eglé Gerulaityté: Courtesy of rider/photo Actionographers, 66–67. **Steph Jeavons:** Courtesy of rider, 68–71.

Tiffani Coates: Courtesy of rider, 7 2–73. **Effie & Avis Hotchkiss:** Harley-Davidson Archives, 74–75. **Jo Rust:** Courtesy of rider, 76–77. **Doris Wiedemann:** Courtesy of rider, 79. **Benka Pulko:** Courtesy of rider/benkapulko.com, 80–81. Linda Bootherstone-Bick: Courtesy of rider, 82–83.

• **RACERS & STUNTERS:** Brandon LaJoie, 84–85. Vicki Golden: Getty Images/Joe Scarnici, 86–87; Getty Images/Tom Pennington, 87. **Debbie Lawler:** Motorbooks archive, 89. **Mercedes Gonzalez:** Courtesy of rider/Racer X archives, 90–91. **Avalon Biddle:** Getty Images/PAUL CROCK/AFP, 92–93; Getty Images/Mirco Lazzari gp, 93. **Tarah Gieger:** Getty Images/Buda Mendes/LatinContent, 94–95; Getty Images/Christian Pondella, 96–97. **Brittney Olsen:** Jeff Cochran, 98; Courtesy of rider, 98–99. **Shelina Moreda:** Alamy Stock Photo/© Matt Cohen/ Southcreek Global/ZUMAPRESS.com, 100T; Getty Images/Mirco Lazzari gp, 101T. Getty Images/Steve Jennings, 100–101B; **Ashley Fiolek:** Getty Images/ Ann Johansson/Corbis, 102–103; Getty Images/ Hyoung Chang/The Denver Post, 103. **Kerry Kleid & Debbi Selden:** Motorbooks archives, 104–105. Melissa Paris: Getty Images/JEAN-FRANCOIS MONIER/ AFP, 106–107. **Vicki Gray:** Courtesy of rider, 108– 109A. **Katja Poensgen:** Getty Images/VANDERLEI ALMEIDA/AFP, 110; Getty Images/Martin Rose/ Bongarts, 111T; Getty Images/GABRIEL BOUYS/AFP, 111B. **Debbie Evans:** Simon Roberts/Shutterstock, 112–113. **Jolene Van Vugt:** Getty Images/Bobby Bank/WireImage, 114–115; Getty Images/Richard Dobson/Newspix, 115. **Erin Sills:** Courtesy of rider, 116. **Marcia Holley:** Kawasaki archive, 117. Shayna Texter: AMA Pro Racing, 118–119. **Kerri Cameron:** Rod Kirkpatrick/fstoppress.com, 120–121. **Ewa

181

ACKNOWLEDGMENTS

I'D LIKE TO THANK EACH AND EVERY WOMAN featured in this book, not just for being inspirational (as if that isn't enough) but for playing a major role in helping me find my place in the world. From Sofi Tsingos, who started as a stranger and now is someone I consider a dear friend, to the Van Buren sisters, whose legendary 1916 cross-country road trip baffled the minds of many. Women who, despite whatever challenges they may face, press on, oftentimes going full throttle at obstacles. It should be noted that no reasonably-sized book could possibly contain the entire collection of incredible history-making moto ladies because there are more breaking records and creating art every day.

They say a rising tide lifts all boats, and the successes of these humans (who happen to be of the female persuasion) are real-world examples of that idea. It wasn't until Kerry Kleid and Debbi Selden went to judicial blows with the AMA in the early 1970s that women were granted racing licenses. Evel Knievel got his ego checked by Debbie Evans in the mid-1970s and created a whole event just to show her up. So as rider and artist Amanda Zito says, "Get out and do the thing." Whatever it is, go for it. You've got a world of women cheering you on—and a lot of fellas, too.

And on a purely personal note, I have just a couple more people to whom I certainly owe my thanks.

When I got an email from Motorbooks talking about wanting to publish a book featuring real women who ride, I quite literally didn't realize they were asking me to write it. As a journalist of over a decade but a complete greenhorn to book publishing, the creative process took some wrestling. I am completely honored to be able to share these stories with the world through the hard work of Motorbooks, my many hours hiding behind a laptop screen, and beautiful images from my personal collection and many of my favorite photographers.

INDEX

183

© 2021 Quarto Publishing Group USA Inc.
Text © 2021 Alicia Mariah Elfving

First Published in 2021 by Motorbooks, an imprint of The Quarto Group, 100 Cummings Center, Suite 265-D, Beverly, MA 01915, USA.
T (978) 282-9590 F (978) 283-2742 QuartoKnows.com

Motorbooks titles are also available at discount for retail, wholesale, promotional, and bulk purchase. For details, contact the Special Sales Manager by email at specialsales@quarto.com or by mail at The Quarto Group, Attn: Special Sales Manager, 100 Cummings Center, Suite 265-D, Beverly, MA 01915, USA.

25 24 23 22 21   1 2 3 4 5

ISBN: 978-0-7603-6750-6

Digital edition published in 2021
eISBN: 978-0-7603-6751-3

Library of Congress Cataloging-in-Publication Data is available.

Creative Direction: Laura Drew
Cover, and interior design: Beth Middleworth
Cover Image: Errol Colandro

Printed in China